MY FAVOURITE CHOCOLATE COOKBOOK

My *Favourite* CHOCOLATE COOKBOOK

Mary Norwak

CASSELL

For

Jonathan   Andrew   Henry
Matthew   Michael   Bertie
and Joseph

who are current and
future chocolate-lovers

A CASSELL BOOK
First published
1993 by Cassell
Villiers House
41/47 Strand
London
WC2N 5JE

Copyright © 1993 Mary Norwak

Designer: Richard Carr

Photographer: Laurie Evans

Jacket Photographer: Sue Atkinson

Distributed in the United States
by Sterling Publishing Co., Inc.
387 Park Avenue South, New York, New York 10016-8810

Distributed in Australia
by Capricorn Link (Australia) Pty Ltd
P.O. Box 665, Lane Cove, NSW 2066

British Library Cataloguing-in-Publication Data
A catalogue record for this book is available from the
British Library

ISBN 0-304-34336-6

Typeset by Litho Link Ltd, Welshpool, Powys, Wales
Printed and bound in Great Britain by Bath Press

CONTENTS

KEY TO RECIPES

★ = Easy
★★ = Fairly easy
★★★ = Needs practice

1

ALL ABOUT CHOCOLATE

WHAT IS THIS CHOCOLATE PASSION, this consuming desire for a simple food which makes strong men weak, and sensible women useless? Why do civilised human beings crave chocolate and risk their money and their weight for sensuous gratification?

Perhaps the answer is that chocolate is not as simple as we think. It is a complex mixture of flavours and textures which provides comfort and nourishment, energy and satisfaction, and that magical quality which lifts the spirit. We eat it for pleasure, tinged with a naughty guilt. We feel wicked as we crunch and munch and wrap our tongues round creamy fillings. We pamper ourselves with the sheer luxury of chocolate, reward our efforts with its comfort, and share its pleasure with our loving friends. Chocolate is handy and accessible, quick and easy to eat, and horribly addictive.

Nobody need feel alone with a chocolate addiction, for sales of chocolate continue to rise. In 1993, over £2 billion was spent on it, supporting an enormous industry employing about 70,000 people who produce the stuff we love. Confectionery is the single largest packaged food market, above milk, bread, tea and coffee, and every Briton gets through an average of 20lb (9kg) of the stuff each year.

Chocolate has come a long way since its beginnings in Central and South America. The Aztecs and Mayans used the cacao bean for a drink consumed at such ceremonial functions as weddings and funerals, and the beans were offered to the gods. In Central America the beans were used as currency, and it was probably here that Columbus discovered them and took them back to Spain where nobody showed interest. Cortés landed in Mexico in 1519, was welcomed by Montezuma the great ruler, and first encountered the royal drink of chocolate or *xocoatl*.

The drink was bitter, but highly spiced and very frothy, and much prized for its energy-giving qualities. Cortés slaughtered the Emperor and destroyed his civilisation, but his soldiers took Mexican seeds of the cocoa trees on their subsequent journey. They planted cocoa trees in Africa on their way home, setting up an industry dominated by the Spaniards as chocolate was slowly introduced to Europe. The Spaniards sweetened their chocolate drinks with sugar and flavoured them with vanilla, bringing chocolate a little nearer to today's luxury.

When the drink first came to Britain, it was introduced through the chocolate house where men gathered in London's Bishopsgate in 1657. For many years chocolate was known only as a drink, made exactly as it had been in earlier times. Lumps of chocolate were broken and soaked in a little warm water until soft. More water was added and the mixture simmered for two hours, then left to get completely cold. Fat settled on the top, which was taken off and discarded. The residual chocolate was then warmed with milk for the final drink, and it was recommended that it should be well beaten when warming so that the drink would thicken. Throughout the eighteenth and nineteenth centuries, doctors recommended chocolate as a restorative for energy and also as a soothing balm for the nerves. At the French court Madame du Barry served cups of reviving chocolate to her suitors, and it is said that Casanova preferred it to champagne.

Perhaps, surprisingly, chocolate took years to develop from a popular drink. In 1728, the first English factory was opened for processing the cocoa bean, but the first solid eating chocolate was not produced until 1847 by Messrs Fry & Sons. Development came more swiftly as the Dutch, Swiss and British worked on new ideas. The earlier and awkward chocolate 'nibs' were converted into simple cocoa liquids and powders; milk chocolate was introduced by the Swiss in 1875, who a few years later perfected the art of making very smooth eating chocolate. By 1900 chocolate was beginning to replace the earlier favourites such as toffee, formerly made in cottage kitchens. Milton Hershey developed his chocolate interests in America, saying 'chocolate is a permanent thing'. His prescience resulted in an American boom in the new confectionery, and today chocoholics gather in Hershey, Pennsylvania, for an annual chocolate festival of five days' indulgence and chocolate bingeing. In France, Switzerland and Britain new confectionery lines were developed after Jules Séchaud produced the first filled chocolate.

Curiously, nobody thought of chocolate or cocoa as a culinary ingredient. It is useless to search in nineteenth-century cookery books for recipes, because chocolate puddings and cakes simply did not exist. The confectioners and *pâtissiers* of middle Europe were the first to develop the luscious chocolate gâteaux and mousses we know today, to serve in their coffee houses with lashings of whipped cream. The taste for chocolate was given another boost as chefs began to finish meals with chocolate delicacies, later taken up by private cooks as the basic ingredients of plain chocolate and cocoa were promoted by manufacturers. Now chocolate is everywhere, easily purchased and easily used, and we may all share the sinful indulgence of the Austrian coffee house.

Chocolate is deliciously indescribable, a mouthwatering experience with a dark, melting, velvety richness. It is for the sybarite who has no wish for Puritan restraint, for the hedonist who doesn't care, for the gourmand with an all-consuming passion.

This book is not for the faint-hearted. It is for the enthusiast who cannot imagine life without chocolate. It is for the cook who always produces something chocolatey among her dinner-party puddings; for the comfort-lover who will order hot chocolate rather than coffee for that mid-morning pick-you-up; for the grown-up schoolboy who always chooses the chocolate cake; for the professed savoury-tooth who can never resist a piece of chocolate cake.

The recipes are the ultimate of their kind – the gooiest cake, the most syrupy sauce, the most sensational fudge, the almost unbelievable roulade and the deepest, fluffiest chocolate soufflé. While the recipes are seductive, they are mostly very simple to achieve. As a chocoholic, one knows that no true believer can spend hours on a complicated recipe because the most important ingredient will be eaten before it reaches the mixing bowl.

2

PRACTICAL MATTERS:

Types of Chocolate and Chocolate Preparation

W HEN PREPARING RECIPES it is important to use the best possible chocolate. If the raw material is of high quality, the resulting dish will be very special. Inferior ingredients produce inferior dishes.

There are many different types of chocolate which may be used, made from cocoa butter, chocolate liquor and sugar, and sometimes milk solids. Their value in cooking depends on the proportion of these essential constituents. In order to be called chocolate, not cake covering, the product must have a minimum of 30 per cent cocoa solids. Some chocolate contains as much as 45 per cent cocoa solids, and this may be checked by reading the packet information. European chocolate tends to be slightly more bitter than British, usually with a more brittle texture. Inevitably, good chocolate is expensive, but well worth spending money on for its depth of flavour, and the cost is usually offset by the relative cheapness of the other ingredients in a chocolate recipe.

Types of Chocolate

Plain Chocolate

This is made from cocoa butter, chocolate liquor, vegetable fats and sugar. It has a good, strong flavour and dark colour, and may be labelled 'bitter', 'fondant' or 'dessert'.

Unsweetened (Bitter) Chocolate

This chocolate is imported and very expensive, and therefore difficult to find. It is totally unsweetened, and it is necessary to adjust the sugar in a recipe to taste. It is sometimes known as 'baker's chocolate'.

Milk Chocolate

Milk chocolate contains cocoa butter, chocolate liquor, vegetable fats and sugar, with milk solids replacing some of the chocolate liquor. It is paler in colour than plain chocolate and has less chocolate flavour, so it is rarely used in recipes.

White Chocolate

Made from cocoa butter, milk and sugar, white chocolate is without colour as it contains no chocolate liquor. It is very sweet with only a light chocolate flavour, and is not easy to melt successfully. It is used in one or two recipes to give contrasting colour, but the flavour is so minimal that it is scarcely worth using.

Couverture

This chocolate for the professional cook contains a very high proportion of cocoa butter. It has a rich flavour, a high sheen and a brittle texture. It has to be tempered by repeated heating and cooling so that it melts successfully, and it is widely used by confectioners.

Chocolate Chips

Small dots of plain or milk chocolate are useful as they melt quickly, and they may be used without melting to provide the chocolate accent in biscuits, cakes and ice creams.

Cake Covering

Often described as 'cooking chocolate', these chocolate-flavoured blocks are made with less than the required minimum of cocoa solids and do not qualify as chocolate. They contain added vegetable and/or coconut oil and do not have a strong flavour. They are, however, cheaper than pure chocolate and have the advantages of melting very easily and of being easy to handle. The chocolate purist will shun a chocolate substitute, but cake covering may be used if cost is more important than flavour.

Cocoa Powder

Unsweetened cocoa powder gives a strong flavour and is useful for baking. The flavour is released by adding a little very hot liquid to the cocoa powder before it is added to a recipe. European cocoa powder has a subtly different flavour, but may be used in the same way.

Drinking Chocolate Powder

This has a subtle chocolate flavour, but it is very sweet, pale and milky and is used only occasionally in baking when other ingredients can be adjusted accordingly.

Chocolate Preparation

Chocolate is not difficult to use, but attention to detail is important as problems can occur which may make dishes unsightly. Particular care is needed in heating and setting chocolate.

Storage

Chocolate should be stored in a cool, dry place, and plain chocolate will store well for a year without loss of colour or flavour (milk chocolate is best used within six months). Chocolate may be stored in a refrigerator or freezer but should be well-wrapped as it tends to pick up other flavours. It may acquire a greyish-white film or bloom because cocoa butter or sugar crystals may rise to the surface after exposure to differing temperatures or excessive moisture. This does not affect the flavour and will disappear after melting.

Chopping and Grating

To speed melting, or to provide small pieces for recipes, chocolate may be chopped or grated. Chocolate may be chopped with a sharp knife or broken up in a food processor. A vegetable peeler or a grater may be used for grating. Be sure that the chocolate is firm and at room temperature before being prepared or it may melt in the hands and be difficult to handle.

Melting

Chocolate is very sensitive to heat and must be melted with great care. If melted on its own, it must be kept completely dry and no hotter than 110°F/44°C. Chocolate should not be melted on its own over direct heat or it will stiffen up and then cannot be reconstituted. There are three ways of melting chocolate successfully.

1. Break the chocolate into small pieces and put them into a bowl or top of a double saucepan. Bring a pan of water to the boil and put the bowl or top saucepan in place, so that the hot water does not touch the bottom of the upper container. Remove from the source of heat so that steam or water does not splash into the chocolate, which will make it seize up and discolour. Stir the chocolate as it melts so that it becomes very smooth. If necessary, reheat the water and replace the bowl or top pan to finish the melting process.

2. Break the chocolate into small pieces and warm in a very low oven (such as the warming oven of a range). The temperature should be no more than 225°F/110°C/Gas ¼.

3. Break the chocolate into small pieces and put into a microwave-proof bowl. Heat for 1–2 minutes in a microwave oven, checking with the manufacturer's instructions if possible. The chocolate will retain its shape but will become soft and smooth when stirred. Remember that foods retain heat and continue warming through after being microwaved, so be careful not to overheat the chocolate.

Do not cover a bowl in which chocolate is being heated, or condensation will form droplets of moisture which will fall back into the chocolate and ruin it.

Liquid may be mixed with chocolate before melting, so that the ingredients are heated together. 1–2 tablespoonsful of water, strong coffee or a spirit such as rum or brandy may be added in this way. If fat is to be added, butter or oil may be stirred in when the chocolate has melted.

Tempering

This is a method of melting chocolate used by professional confectioners to give a perfect finish to their work. The chocolate used has a high proportion of cocoa butter and is repeatedly heated and cooled so that it finally melts and sets perfectly. This is not necessary with the eating chocolate generally used which has a lower proportion of cocoa butter.

Setting

Chocolate sets best at a fairly cool temperature of 65°F/18°C, but will set at a room temperature of about 72°F/22°C. At this higher temperature, setting will take a little longer, but the chocolate will retain its shape and shine. Do not try to set chocolate in a refrigerator as it develops a white bloom; choose a reasonably cool, dry place instead.

Dipping

If using chocolate to coat sweets or fruit, be sure to melt it in a wide bowl for easy use. Cool the chocolate to 92–110°F/33–44°C so that it is still liquid but will adhere to the object being dipped. For a smooth, shiny finish, add 1 tablespoon vegetable oil to 6oz (175g) chocolate.

Use a cocktail stick, skewer, fondue fork or confectionery fork to dip the items concerned; allow excess chocolate to drip off, and push off the dipped object with another skewer or cocktail stick. If items are placed on foil or baking parchment, they can be easily removed.

Moulding

Chocolate may be moulded in plastic, metal or paper moulds. They should be completely dry and clean so that the chocolate will not stick and crack. Polish plastic or metal moulds with a piece of kitchen paper so that the chocolate remains very shiny, and do not handle finished chocolates with the fingers as they mark quickly.

Substitution of Chocolate

If a small quantity of chocolate is needed for a recipe and is not available, it is possible to substitute 3 tablespoons cocoa powder, ½oz (15g) butter and 1 tablespoon sugar for each 1oz (25g) chocolate.

Making Mistakes

When chocolate is overheated, or when cold liquid such as water or cream is added to hot chocolate, it will 'seize' and become cloudy, dull and lumpy. It will usually have to be discarded, but it may be possible to rectify the situation by stirring in a little vegetable oil.

3

COMPLEMENTARY FLAVOURS

THERE IS A GREAT ART in improving and enhancing a dish by complementary flavouring. Cookery experts like to keep their flavouring secrets closely guarded, because knowing 'what goes with what' lifts their cooking out of the common rut. Complementary flavourings are meant to accent a dish and give it greater depth and complexity without smothering its basic flavour. Skilful use of these flavourings improves dishes beyond all recognition, and the cook's palate needs to be finely tuned to get the combinations right and to avoid the bad restaurant disaster of hare-and-apricots-wrapped-in-spinach-in-redcurrant-sauce-served-with-a-chocolate-biscuit type. Quantities of complementary flavourings are difficult to prescribe; successful results can only be gauged by the fineness of the creator's palate, and by the people who eat the finished dish.

Chocolate is a magnificent basic ingredient, strongly flavoured and stamping its own character on any dish which includes it. Even so, a chocolate recipe can be flat, dull and cloying without a hint of liqueur, a touch of spice or a surprise of fruit. The following list gives guidance on those flavourings which are the finest complements to chocolate.

Nuts

The soft melting smoothness of chocolate is greatly enhanced by the crunch of nuts, particularly *walnuts*, *hazelnuts*, *almonds*, *pecans*, *Brazils* and *coconut*. An extra dimension is given when the nuts are lightly toasted or caramelised.

Caramel

The slightly burnt sugar flavouring of caramel is a fine foil for chocolate, probably at its best when nut praline is used in recipes.

Dried Fruit

The softness of dried fruit blends with chocolate and adds a light sweetness. Use *raisins*, *sultanas*, *candied peel* or *glacé fruit*. The texture and flavour are improved if the fruits are soaked in a little spirit, such as rum or brandy, before using in a recipe.

Spirits and Liqueurs

A few drops of liqueur lift a chocolate mousse, a cake filling or a sauce to a different plane. There is no need to drown a dish in alcohol, and this is particularly important when a dish is not heated to remove the alcoholic effect. *Rum*, *brandy* and *whisky* accent chocolate and add a light flavouring of their own. More distinctive flavouring is given by liqueurs based on *coffee*, *chocolate*, *mint*, *orange*, *raspberry*, *blackcurrant* and *cherry*.

Herbs and Spices

The combination of spice and chocolate is an old one, perhaps because they come from the same hot climate. The classics which enhance chocolate are *cinnamon*, *ginger* and *vanilla*. In a cooler climate, *peppermint* is a traditional accompaniment, giving a teasing sparkle to the heaviness of very dark chocolate. When using this flavouring, choose peppermint oil, rather than essence, which has a flat, synthetic flavour.

Fruit

The paradoxical sharp sweetness of fruit goes wonderfully with chocolate. Fresh fruit may be used in many dishes, while fruit jams make the perfect foil to chocolate cake. Use *pears*, *oranges*, *raspberries*, *strawberries*, *blackcurrants*, *apricots*, *cherries* and *pineapple*. For tremendous sophistication, try *cranberries*.

Coffee

Coffee and chocolate have an extraordinary relationship, and one which is as ancient and traditional as that of spice and chocolate, probably for the same reason that the two ingredients came from similar climates and areas of the world. The combination is usually known as *mocha*, and it will be found that a hint of coffee enhances a chocolate dish, just as a little chocolate gives depth to a coffee recipe. The flavouring may be introduced by using coffee liqueur, very strong black coffee, coffee essence or coffee powder.

Chocolate and Wine

Chocolate provides real problems for the wine-lover, and it is notoriously difficult to partner with wine at the end of a meal. One solution for the strong-hearted is to offer a small glass of *Armagnac* or *rum* which will complement the dish. Those who dislike spirits will have a greater problem in coping with the sweetness of the chocolate and its mouth-coating texture. A compromise may be a fortified wine such as *Málaga* or *port*, which contain a stiffening of brandy.

Traditional champagne and the sweet muscat dessert wines are not good partners for chocolate. General consensus seems to be in favour of simple but characterful wines, which need to be good ones to stand up to the chocolate. A good *Sauternes* or *asti spumante* seems to work well, and so surprisingly do some dry red wines. It is a good idea to experiment before offering a wine and chocolate combination, and if in doubt, leave the idea alone. Serve the cheese course with its appropriate wine before the pudding, and then serve the chocolate dish and follow up with a good cup of coffee.

4

CHOCOLATE CLASSICS

A FEW CHOCOLATE RECIPES have achieved the status of classic dishes. Mostly of French and Austrian origin, they are triumphs of the *pâtissier*'s art, which look delectable and often complicated, and which are fine examples of the skills of combining flavours and textures to produce a perfect and altogether elegant result.

Nobody need be frightened of trying to reproduce these classic dishes. All *pâtisserie* consists of a number of relatively simple recipes combined in a unique way. If a cook can make a reasonable sponge cake, meringue, shortbread, butter icing, fruit glaze and caramel, the delicious recipes in this chapter may be easily achieved. The essential ingredient is time to make each component part as perfect as possible.

Chocolate Marquise
★★

This is a very light mousse but the flavour is intense and rich, since both chocolate and cocoa powder are used. Every chef has a personal recipe for Marquise, usually a closely-guarded secret.

Ingredients
FOR 6–8

7oz (200g) plain chocolate
3¹/₂oz (90g) unsalted butter
3oz (75g) caster sugar
1oz (25g) cocoa powder
3 egg yolks
2 tbs rum or brandy
¹/₂pt (300ml) double cream

Line a 1lb (450g) loaf tin with foil, smoothing down the creases carefully.

Break the chocolate into small pieces and put into a bowl over a pan of hot water. When the chocolate has melted, remove from heat and leave to cool. Whip the butter and half the sugar until very pale and creamy and work in the cocoa powder. Whisk the egg yolks and remaining sugar until almost white and very fluffy, and then whisk in the rum or brandy. Whip the cream to soft peaks.

Add the chocolate to the butter mixture and mix well. Gradually work in the egg mixture and finally fold in the cream. Pour into the prepared tin and chill for 4 hours. Turn out on to a serving dish. Serve in slices with any of the sauces on pp109–13.

Dobos Torte

★★★

This marvellous cake consists of thin layers of sponge sandwiched with chocolate cream, with the surface covered with a thick layer of caramel. It is a triumph of the Hungarian kitchen and used to be a speciality of Floris in Soho. It was always chosen for birthday celebrations by the staff of *Vogue* magazine.

Ingredients

FOR AN 8IN (20CM) CAKE

8oz (225g) unsalted butter
8oz (225g) caster sugar
4 eggs
6oz (175g) self-raising flour
½ tsp baking powder
pinch of salt

FILLING

6oz (175g) sugar
5 tbs water
2 egg yolks
6oz (175g) unsalted butter
4oz (100g) plain chocolate

CARAMEL

3oz (75g) sugar
3 tbs water

Preheat the oven to 400°F/200°C/Gas 6. Grease three 8in (20cm) sandwich tins and dust lightly with flour. Beat the butter and sugar together until very light and creamy. Separate the eggs and beat in the yolks one at a time. Sieve together the flour, baking powder and salt and fold into the mixture. Whisk the egg whites to stiff peaks and fold into the mixture.

Using half the mixture, spread thin layers in each sandwich tin and bake for 8 minutes until golden brown. Allow to cool in the tins for 2 minutes and turn on to wire racks to cool. Re-grease and flour the tins and bake the remaining mixture to make six layers in all.

To make the filling, put the sugar and water into a heavy-based pan and heat gently until the sugar has dissolved. Bring to the boil and boil to 215°F/102°C, until the syrup spins a short fine thread from a spoon. Whisk the egg yolks in a bowl until thick and creamy and gradually beat in the hot syrup until the mixture is cool and fluffy. In a separate bowl, beat the butter until soft and light and add the egg mixture a little at a time, beating until smooth and shiny. Melt the chocolate in a bowl over hot water and beat into the mixture. Refrigerate while preparing the caramel.

To make the caramel, put the sugar and water into a heavy-based pan and stir over low heat until the sugar has dissolved. Bring to the boil and boil to 345°F/174°C, when the syrup will be clear and caramel-coloured. Spread this caramel evenly over the top of one cake layer, using an oiled knife. While still soft, mark into eight triangles with a sharp knife and leave to set.

Assemble the cake layers and chocolate cream on a serving dish, making each cream layer the same depth as each cake layer. Top with the caramel-covered layer and pipe any spare chocolate cream in whorls round the edge.

COOK'S TIP
FOR MAKING BUTTERCREAM

As soon as the syrup has reached the required temperature, remove from the heat. It is best to use an electric beater so that the syrup can be poured on to the eggs while beating continues. The egg yolks must be thick and creamy and the syrup must be added in a thin trickle. The butter should be at room temperature so that it can be beaten to a soft light creaminess.

Marjolaine
★★★

A truly wonderful cake made from layers of nutty sponge with chocolate cream, coffee cream and praline cream, finished with more praline. The assembly is a little complicated but each stage of the preparation is easy, so that the cook only needs time to be successful.

Ingredients
FOR ONE 9x6IN (22.5x15CM) CAKE

8oz (225g) almonds
4oz (100g) hazelnuts
8oz (225g) caster sugar
1 tbs plain flour
1 tbs cocoa powder
8 egg whites

FILLING

8oz (225g) sugar
¼pt (150ml) water
8oz (225g) unsalted butter
3 tbs brandy
3 egg yolks
2oz (50g) plain chocolate
1 tbs strong black coffee

PRALINE

8oz (225g) almonds
4oz (100g) sugar
2 tbs water

Preheat the oven to 400°F/200°C/Gas 6. Butter and flour two 12x9in (30x22.5cm) Swiss-roll tins. Dip the almonds into boiling water and slip off their skins. Grill the hazelnuts and rub off the skins. Mix the almonds and hazelnuts and grill until golden brown. Grind in a blender until fine and stir with 7oz (200g) sugar, the flour and cocoa powder until evenly coloured. Whisk the egg whites to stiff peaks and gradually beat in the remaining sugar. Fold in the nut mixture. Spread over Swiss-roll tins and bake for 15 minutes. Cool in the tins for 5 minutes and then cool on a wire rack. Cut each cake in half.

To prepare the filling, put the sugar and water into a pan and boil to 240°F/116°C, when a little of the mixture dropped into cold water forms a soft ball. Take off the heat and cool to lukewarm. Beat the butter until very soft and light and gradually beat in the syrup, brandy and egg yolks. Divide the mixture in half and divide one half into half again. Melt the chocolate in a bowl over hot water and beat into one of the smaller portions. Flavour the other small portion with the coffee.

Prepare the praline by blanching the almonds in hot water and then grilling them until golden brown. Put the sugar and water into a heavy-based pan and simmer until it just begins to colour. Stir in the nuts until well coated and when the syrup is caramel colour, pour on to an oiled plate or marble slab. When cold, break into pieces and grind in a blender or food processor.

Fold half the praline into the large portion of filling. Put one cake on to a serving plate and spread with chocolate filling. Top with a second cake and spread with coffee filling. Top with the third cake and spread with half the praline filling. Top with the final cake and spread with remaining filling. Sprinkle with the remaining praline. Chill for 30 minutes before serving.

Bûche de Noël

★★★

This chocolate Swiss roll with a rich chocolate filling and icing is the traditional French Christmas cake. The centre can also be filled with chestnut purée mixed with whipped cream and flavoured with orange liqueur for something extra special.

Ingredients
FOR ONE LOG CAKE

4 eggs
4oz (100g) caster sugar
3oz (75g) self-raising flour
1oz (25g) cocoa powder

FILLING AND ICING

3oz (75g) sugar
5 tbs water
4 egg yolks
6oz (175g) unsalted butter
3oz (75g) plain chocolate
2 tbs rum
a little icing sugar

Preheat the oven to 400°F/200°C/Gas 6. Grease and base-line a 12x9in (30x22.5cm) Swiss-roll tin. Whisk the eggs and sugar together until pale, thick and creamy. Sieve together the flour and cocoa powder and fold into the egg mixture. Spread in the prepared tin and bake for 12 minutes. Turn out on to a piece of greaseproof paper sprinkled with caster sugar. Peel off the lining paper. Trim the edges of the cake and roll up firmly with the paper inside. Cover with a clean tea cloth and leave until cold.

To make the filling, put the sugar and water into a heavy-based pan and heat gently until the sugar has dissolved. Bring to the boil and boil to 215°F/102°C, until the syrup spins a short fine thread from a spoon (see Cook's Tip, p.22). Whisk the egg yolks in a bowl until thick and creamy and gradually beat in the hot syrup until the mixture is cool and fluffy. In a separate bowl, beat the butter until soft and light and add the egg mixture a little at a time, beating until smooth and shiny. Melt the chocolate in a bowl over hot water and beat into the mixture with the rum.

Unroll the cake and spread with one-third of the filling mixture. Roll up and place on a serving dish or board. Cover with the remaining mixture and mark with a fork to look like a log. Chill for 1 hour. Just before serving, sprinkle with a little icing sugar to look like snow and decorate with robins and holly.

Devil's Food

★★★

An American favourite which combines a dense, dark chocolate cake with a white fluffy frosting. There is also Angel Food, which by contrast is a pure white cake.

Ingredients
FOR AN 8IN (20CM) CAKE

8oz (225g) light soft brown sugar
2oz (50g) cocoa powder
¼pt (150ml) milk
4oz (100g) unsalted butter
2 eggs
8oz (225g) plain flour
1 teasp bicarbonate of soda

ICING

1lb (450g) sugar
¼pt (150ml) water
2 egg whites

Preheat the oven to 325°F/160°C/Gas 3. Grease and line an 8in (20cm) round cake tin. Put the sugar, cocoa powder and milk into a pan with the butter. Heat gently until the butter and sugar have melted and the mixture is smooth. Leave until just cold. Beat in the eggs. Sieve the flour and bicarbonate of soda and beat into the mixture. Pour into the tin and bake for 1 hour. Cool in the tin for 5 minutes and turn on to a wire rack to cool. When cold, split into three layers.

To make the icing, put the sugar and water into a heavy-based pan and stir over low heat until the sugar has dissolved. Boil to 240°F/116°C, when a little of the mixture dropped into cold water forms a soft ball. Whisk the egg whites to stiff peaks. Pour in the hot syrup gradually, whisking all the time, and continue whisking until the icing is thick and stands in soft peaks. Sandwich together the cake layers with this mixture and spread the remaining icing all over the cake. Leave to stand for 30 minutes before serving.

COOK'S TIP
FOR MAKING ICING

When making the icing, remove the syrup from the heat as soon as the correct temperature is reached. Add the syrup to the egg whites in a thin trickle, whisking all the time. Use the icing as soon as the mixture is thick and softly peaked.

Cassata
★★

This Sicilian confection is a fluffy combination of cheese with fruit peel and chocolate, wrapped in sponge cake and finished with chocolate – not the often debased version, which is just a mixture of ice cream and candied peel.

Ingredients
FOR 8

1lb (450g) curd cheese
2oz (50g) caster sugar
4 tbs orange liqueur
4oz (100g) chopped mixed candied peel
2oz (50g) plain chocolate
8 trifle sponges

ICING

6oz (175g) plain chocolate
3 tbs strong black coffee
3oz (75g) unsalted butter

Line a 2pt (1.2l) pudding basin with foil. Press and smooth down the creases carefully.

Cream the cheese and sugar together until light and fluffy and work in half the liqueur. Add the peel. Chop the chocolate finely and fold into the mixture.

Split the trifle sponges in half and sprinkle the cut sides with the remaining liqueur. Line the base and sides of the basin with the sponge, cut-sides inwards, reserving a few pieces for the top. Fill with the cheese mixture and cover with remaining sponge. Cover and chill for 12 hours. Turn on to a serving dish.

To make the icing, put the chocolate and coffee into a bowl over a pan of hot water and heat gently until the chocolate has melted. Remove from heat and beat in small pieces of butter. Cool and spread over the pudding. Chill for 1 hour before serving.

Sacher Torte

***

The pride of Vienna, this rich, light chocolate sponge is glazed with apricot jam before being finished with a smooth chocolate glaze. It is often served with a mountain of whipped cream.

Ingredients
FOR A 9IN (22.5CM) CAKE

8oz (225g) plain chocolate
1 tbs rum
8oz (225g) unsalted butter
8oz (225g) caster sugar
5 eggs
6oz (175g) self-raising flour

FILLING AND ICING

4 tbs apricot jam
4oz (100g) plain chocolate
4oz (100g) caster sugar
3tbs water
2 drops olive oil

Grease and line a 9in (22.5cm) round tin. Preheat the oven to 300°F/150°C/Gas 2. Melt the chocolate with the rum in a bowl over hot water and leave to cool. Cream the butter and sugar until light and fluffy. Separate the eggs and beat in the yolks one at a time, then the melted chocolate. Sieve the flour and fold into the mixture. Whisk the egg whites to stiff peaks and fold into the chocolate mixture. Put into prepared tin and bake for 1½ hours. Leave in the tin for 15 minutes and turn on to a wire rack to cool. When cold, split into two layers. Sieve the jam and warm it slightly. With half the jam sandwich the layers together and brush the rest all over the cake.

To make the icing, melt the chocolate in a pan over hot water and leave until cool. Put the water and sugar into a heavy-based pan and simmer until the syrup is straw-coloured. Cool to lukewarm and stir into the chocolate. Add the oil and beat well. Smooth all over the cake. Leave to set for 1 hour.

Black Forest Gâteau

***

A tempting mixture of chocolate sponge, slightly sharp cherries, kirsch, cream and plain chocolate – very different from some of the versions served in a cheap restaurant meal. It is not difficult to make, but needs a little time and care.

Ingredients
FOR A 9IN (22.5CM) CAKE

5oz (125g) plain chocolate
2 tbs water
5oz (125g) unsalted butter
5oz (125g) caster sugar
4 eggs and 1 egg white
2oz (50g) self-raising flour

FILLING

1½lb (675g) canned morello cherries in syrup
1 tbs arrowroot
6 tbs kirsch
¾pt (450ml) double cream
1oz (25g) icing sugar
chocolate curls (p122)

Preheat the oven to 400°F/200°C/Gas 6. Butter a 9in (22.5cm) spring-form tin and sprinkle evenly with flour. Break the chocolate into small pieces and put into a bowl with the water. Melt over a pan of hot water and leave to cool. Cream the butter and sugar until very pale and light. Separate the eggs and beat the yolks one at a time into the butter. Beat in the flour and then the melted chocolate. Whisk the egg whites to stiff peaks and fold into the cake mixture. Put into the prepared tin and bake for 40 minutes. Turn off the oven and leave the cake in for 5 minutes. Remove from the oven and cool in the tin for 15 minutes before turning on to a wire rack to finish cooling. When cold, cut the cake in half to make two layers and put the base on to a serving dish.

Drain the cherries and mix 2 tbs of the syrup with 2 tbs kirsch. Sprinkle over the cut sides of the cake layers. Mix the arrowroot with 3 tbs cherry syrup. Heat the remaining syrup just to boiling point. Mix with the arrowroot and then reheat gently until thick. Take off the heat.

Stone the cherries and reserve 12 for decoration. Stir the rest into the sauce with half the remaining kirsch. Leave until cold. Whip the cream and icing sugar to soft peaks and fold in the remaining kirsch. Spread the bottom cake layer with the cherry mixture and one-third of the cream. Add the top cake layer. Spread the remaining cream lightly all over the cake. Decorate with the reserved cherries and plenty of chocolate curls. Chill for 1 hour before serving.

Nègre en Chemise
★★

A wonderfully rich steamed chocolate pudding, which gets its name from the dark centre in a 'shirt' of white cream.

Ingredients
FOR 6

4oz (100g) white bread without crusts
¼pt (150ml) double cream
3oz (75g) plain chocolate
4oz (100g) unsalted butter
3oz (75g) caster sugar
2oz (50g) ground almonds
4 eggs
¼pt (150ml) whipping cream
½oz (15g) icing sugar

Grease a 2pt (1.2l) pudding basin. Break the bread into small pieces and put into a bowl with the cream. Leave to stand for 15 minutes and mash lightly with a fork. Break the chocolate into small pieces and put into a bowl over pan of hot water. Heat gently until melted.

Cream the butter and sugar until light and fluffy and beat in the almonds, eggs and melted chocolate. Gradually beat in the bread mixture until evenly coloured. Put into the prepared basin, cover with foil and steam for 2 hours.

Whip the whipping cream and icing sugar to soft peaks. Turn the pudding on to a serving dish. Spoon the cream over it and serve at once.

Chocolate Eclairs

★★

This cunning combination of crisp light casing, sweetened cream and a dark chocolate glaze is perhaps the most indulgent of all chocolate-based cakes.

Ingredients
FOR 12 ÉCLAIRS

2¹/₂oz (65g) plain flour
pinch of salt
2oz (50g) butter
¹/₄pt (150ml) water
2 eggs and 1 egg yolk

FILLING AND ICING

¹/₂pt (300ml) double cream
1 egg white
¹/₂oz (15g) icing sugar
6oz (175g) plain chocolate

Preheat the oven to 400°F/200°C/Gas 6. Rinse two baking sheets in cold water. Sieve the flour and salt together. Put the butter and water into a pan and bring to the boil. Tip in the flour quickly and beat hard over low heat until the mixture is smooth; cook for 1 minute until it leaves the sides of the pan cleanly. Cool to lukewarm and then beat in the eggs a little at a time until the mixture is smooth and shiny. Make sure the baking sheets are still wet, and pipe the mixture into 3in (7.5cm) lengths on to them, leaving room for expansion. Bake for 25 minutes. Slit each éclair with a sharp knife and return to the oven for 5 minutes to dry out. Cool on a wire rack.

Whip the cream to stiff peaks. Whisk the egg white to stiff peaks and then whisk in the icing sugar. Fold into the cream. Slit right along the side of each éclair and fill with cream.

Break the chocolate into small pieces and put into a bowl over a pan of hot water. Heat until melted. Dip the top of each éclair into the chocolate and leave to set. Serve freshly baked.

COOK'S TIP
FOR MAKING ÉCLAIRS

It is important to follow the recipe very carefully to achieve perfect éclairs. Be sure not to open the oven door when baking. Don't fill and ice the éclairs until just before serving so that they retain their crispness.

5

HOT PUDDINGS

A FTER A TRADITIONAL family Sunday lunch when a simple roast joint, poultry or game has been served, a hot chocolate pudding is a special treat and brings a triumphant note to the end of the meal. For those with more delicate digestions, it is best to serve such a pudding after a very simple and not very filling salad.

Many of these puddings contain their own built-in sauce, but if they do not they may be paired with one of the many delicious suggestions on pp109–13, or with cream or ice cream.

Hot Chocolate Meringue Pudding
*

A truly yummy pudding which makes a special treat for a family Sunday lunch and is easy to make.

Ingredients
FOR 4

4 oz (100g) plain chocolate
1oz (25g) butter
1oz (25g) sugar
½pt (300ml) milk
2oz (50g) fresh white breadcrumbs
2oz (50g) seedless raisins
2 eggs
4oz (100g) caster sugar

Preheat the oven to 350°F/180°C/Gas 4. Grease a 1½pt (900ml) pie dish.

Break the chocolate into small pieces and put into a pan with the butter, sugar and milk. Heat gently until the chocolate and butter have melted. Mix the breadcrumbs and raisins in a bowl and pour in the hot liquid. Mix well and leave until lukewarm. Separate the eggs and beat the yolks into the chocolate mixture. Pour into the pie dish and bake for 30 minutes. Whisk the egg whites to stiff peaks and fold in the caster sugar. Pile on top of the pudding and bake for 10 minutes. Serve at once with cream.

Chocolate Cream Pancakes

Thin chocolate-flavoured pancakes filled with flavoured cream and topped with rich chocolate sauce. Prepare the pancakes in advance and keep them warm and ready for quick assembly.

Ingredients

For 4

4oz (100g) plain flour
2 eggs
½pt (300ml) milk
1 tbs drinking chocolate powder
pinch of salt
1 tbs oil
lard for frying

FILLING

2oz (50g) seedless raisins
2 tbs rum
2oz (50g) walnuts
½pt (300ml) double cream

½pt (300ml) Chocolate Sauce (p109)

Put the flour into a bowl and gradually whisk in the eggs, milk, drinking chocolate powder, salt and oil. Using lard, fry 8 thin pancakes until golden on each side.

While the pancakes are being fried, leave the raisins to soak in the rum. Chop the walnuts and add to the raisins. Whip the cream to soft peaks and fold in the raisins, walnuts and rum. Just before serving, wrap each pancake round some of the cream mixture. Serve at once with Chocolate Sauce.

Chocolate Walnut Pudding

This very light steamed chocolate pudding studded with walnuts can be served with *Dark Chocolate Rum Sauce (p111)* or whipped cream.

Ingredients

For 6

2oz (50g) plain chocolate
3oz (75g) unsalted butter
3oz (75g) caster sugar
1 egg
4oz (100g) fresh white breadcrumbs
2oz (50g) self-raising flour
few drops of vanilla essence
5 tbs milk
2oz (50g) walnuts

Grease a 1½pt (900ml) pudding basin. Break the chocolate into a bowl over a pan of hot water and heat gently until the chocolate has melted. Cream the butter and sugar until light and fluffy. Work in the melted chocolate. Separate the egg and beat the yolk into the chocolate mixture. Stir in the breadcrumbs, flour, essence and milk. Chop the nuts roughly and add to the mixture. Whisk the egg white to stiff peaks and fold into the mixture.

Put into the pudding basin and cover with greaseproof paper and foil. Put into a pan of boiling water with the water coming half-way up the bowl. Cover and cook for 1¾ hours, adding more boiling water to the pan from time to time so that the pan does not boil dry. Unmould on to a warm serving dish and serve at once.

Saucy Mocha Pudding

*

This chocolate-coffee baked pudding with its own sauce makes a superb finish to a Sunday lunch.

Ingredients
FOR 4

4oz (100g) self-raising flour
1oz (25g) drinking chocolate powder
4oz (100g) butter
3oz (75g) caster sugar
2 eggs

SAUCE

1 tbs drinking chocolate powder
2 teasp coffee powder
1 tbs cornflour
2 tbs light soft brown sugar
½ teasp ground cinnamon
½pt (300ml) water
1oz (25g) butter
caster sugar

Preheat the oven to 375°F/190°F/Gas 5. Grease a 2½pt (1.5l) ovenware dish. Stir the flour and drinking chocolate powder together until evenly coloured. Cream the butter and sugar together until light and fluffy, and work in the eggs alternately with the flour. Spoon into the dish and smooth the top lightly.

Mix the drinking chocolate powder, coffee powder, cornflour, soft brown sugar and cinnamon together in a heavy-based pan, and mix in the water. Bring to the boil, stirring well. Stir in the butter. Pour over the pudding mixture.

Bake for 1 hour. Leave to stand for 5 minutes and then sprinkle with caster sugar. Serve at once on its own or with whipped cream if liked.

Hot Chocolate Betty

*

A 'Betty' is a layered pudding of bread-crumbs and fruit, and this version is a wonderful blend of delicate pears with chocolate and cinnamon.

Ingredients
FOR 4

1lb (450g) ripe eating pears
6oz (175g) white or brown breadcrumbs
3oz (75g) light soft brown sugar
½ lemon
1 teasp ground cinnamon
2oz (50g) grated plain chocolate
2 tbs golden syrup
2oz (50g) butter

Preheat the oven to 375°F/190°C/Gas 5. Grease a 2pt (1.2l) ovenware dish. Peel, core and slice the pears, and put half of them in the dish. Mix the breadcrumbs with 2oz (50g) sugar, grated lemon rind, cinnamon and chocolate. Sprinkle half the mixture on the pears. Cover with the remaining pears and top with the remaining crumb mixture. Squeeze out the lemon juice and heat gently with the syrup. Pour over the breadcrumbs and sprinkle with the remaining sugar. Cut the butter into flakes and arrange on top of the pudding. Bake for 40 minutes. Serve hot or cold with cream.

Chocolate Apricot Crumble

*

Chocolate is a delicious enhancer of the humble crumble. Apricots make the nicest filling, but it is worth trying raspberries or black cherries.

Ingredients
FOR 4

12oz (350g) dried apricots
2oz (50g) walnuts
4oz (100g) plain flour
3oz (75g) unsalted butter
3oz (75g) light soft brown sugar
3oz (75g) chocolate chips
cream

Soak the apricots in water to cover for 2–3 hours. Simmer gently until just tender. Chop the apricots roughly and mix with the chopped walnuts. Put into a greased ovenware dish. Sieve the flour into a bowl and rub in the butter until the mixture is like fine breadcrumbs. Stir in the sugar and chocolate chips. Sprinkle over the fruit but do not press down. Bake at 350°F/180°C/ Gas 4 for 45 minutes. Serve hot or cold with cream.

Chocolate Fondue

*

An easy pudding for the chocolate addict which is good for an informal party. Be sure to have a wide variety of dipping items as some people like very sweet things, while others prefer the contrasting sharpness of fruit.

Ingredients
FOR 4–6

8oz (225g) plain chocolate
½pt (300ml) double cream
1–2 tbs rum or brandy
marshmallows, peppermint creams, pieces of fresh fruit

Break the chocolate into small pieces and put into a fondue dish or into a bowl over a pan of hot water. Add the cream and heat gently, stirring frequently until the chocolate has melted. Stir in the rum or brandy. Keep warm and use fondue forks or chopsticks for dipping in sweets and fruit.

Types of Chocolate and Decorations
Dobos Torte (p22)
Chocolate Eclairs (p28)
Hot Chocolate Soufflé (p36)

Chocolate Eggy Bread
*

The old nursery favourite with a special chocolate flavour is served to grown-ups with a lightly alcoholic sauce.

Ingredients
FOR 4–6

½pt (300ml) milk
1oz (25g) drinking chocolate powder
1 egg
6 large thick white bread slices
oil for frying
2oz (50g) caster sugar
1 teasp ground cinnamon

JAM SAUCE

8 tbs apricot jam
2 tbs rum

Put the milk and drinking chocolate powder into a pan and heat to just under boiling point, whisking to mix well. Take off the heat and cool to lukewarm. Beat in the egg. Trim the crusts from the bread and cut each piece into three rectangles. Dip each piece into the chocolate mixture and fry at once in hot shallow oil. Drain well on kitchen paper. Mix the caster sugar and cinnamon until evenly coloured and sprinkle on the fried slices.

Melt the jam, remove from heat and stir in the rum. Serve the chocolate slices very hot with the hot jam sauce.

Rum Hazelnut Pudding
*

This rich version of a steamed chocolate pudding is wonderful served hot with a bowl of whipped cream lightly flavoured with rum.

Ingredients
FOR 6

4oz (100g) plain chocolate
5oz (125g) butter
3oz (75g) caster sugar
5 eggs
2 tbs rum
3oz (75g) ground almonds
3oz (75g) ground toasted hazelnuts
3oz (75g) sultanas
3 tbs dry breadcrumbs

Grease a 2pt (1.2l) pudding basin with a little of the butter and sprinkle with a little of the sugar. Break the chocolate into a small bowl and put over a pan of hot water until melted. Cream the butter and sugar until light and fluffy. Separate the eggs and beat the yolks into the creamed mixture with the rum and melted chocolate. Stir in the almonds, hazelnuts, sultanas and bread-crumbs. Whisk the egg whites to stiff peaks and fold into the mixture.

Pour into the prepared basin and cover with a piece of greaseproof paper and a piece of foil, tying firmly with string. Put into a pan of boiling water to come half-way up the pudding basin. Cover and steam for 1½ hours, adding more boiling water to the pan if necessary. Turn on to a warm serving dish and serve at once.

Chocolate Fudge Pudding

*

A rich dark chocolate sauce forms under the cake-like top of this pudding, which is strictly for chocoholics. It is best served just warm, with cream or ice cream.

Ingredients
FOR 6

6oz (175g) granulated sugar
4oz (100g) plain flour
2 teasp baking powder
pinch of salt
1oz (25g) plain chocolate
1oz (25g) butter
¼pt (150ml) milk

TOPPING

4oz (100g) caster sugar
3oz (75g) light soft brown sugar
3 heaped tbs cocoa powder
6 tbs water

Preheat the oven to 325°F/160°C/Gas 3. Grease a 1½pt (900ml) ovenware dish. Stir together the sugar, flour, baking powder and salt. Put the chocolate, butter and milk into a small saucepan and heat until the chocolate has melted. Leave until cool and then beat into the dry ingredients. Spread in the prepared dish.

Sprinkle on top the sugars, cocoa powder and water without mixing. Bake for 1 hour. Leave to stand at room temperature for 1 hour before serving.

Chocolate Almond Pudding

*

A sophisticated steamed pudding which is very good served with whipped cream flavoured with a little rum or brandy.

Ingredients
FOR 6

4oz (100g) unsalted butter
4oz (100g) icing sugar
4oz (100g) plain chocolate
4oz (100g) ground almonds
6 eggs

Well grease a 2pt (900ml) pudding basin with butter and sprinkle with a little caster sugar. Cream the butter and icing sugar until light and fluffy. Grate the chocolate and work into the butter mixture with the almonds. Separate the eggs and beat the yolks into the mixture until it is very soft and light.

Whisk the egg whites to stiff peaks and fold into the chocolate mixture. Spoon into the prepared basin and cover with greased greaseproof paper and foil. Steam for 1 hour. Turn out on to a warm serving dish and serve at once.

Chocolate Upside-Down Pudding

The slight sharpness of pineapple contrasts with a rich chocolate baked pudding, served with *Chocolate Sauce (p109)*.

Ingredients
FOR 6

4oz (100g) unsalted butter
4oz (100g) caster sugar
2 eggs
2 tbs milk
5oz (125g) self-raising flour
1oz (25g) cocoa powder

TOPPING

2oz (50g) unsalted butter
2oz (50g) caster sugar
7 pineapple rings
7 glacé cherries
2oz (50g) walnuts

Preheat the oven to 350°F/180°C/Gas 4. Grease an 8in (20cm) round cake tin. Prepare the topping first by creaming the butter and sugar together and spreading over the base of the cake tin. Place the pineapple rings on top, with a glacé cherry in the centre of each. Chop the walnuts roughly and sprinkle in the tin.

Cream the butter and sugar. Beat the eggs and milk together. Sieve the flour and cocoa powder. Add the eggs and flour alternately to the creamed mixtured, beating well between each addition. Spoon over the pineapple rings. Bake for 50 minutes. Leave to stand in tin for 5 minutes and turn on to a warm serving dish. Serve at once with hot Chocolate Sauce.

White Chocolate Pudding

A pale golden steamed pudding with a chocolate flavour to serve with an enticing *Dark Chocolate Rum Sauce (p111)*.

Ingredients
FOR 4–6

4oz (100g) white chocolate
4oz (100g) unsalted butter
4oz (100g) caster sugar
2 eggs
4oz (100g) plain flour
pinch of salt
2 tbs milk
½ teasp vanilla essence

Break the chocolate into small pieces and put into a bowl over a pan of hot water. Heat gently until melted. Cream the butter and sugar until light and fluffy. Beat the eggs together. Sieve the flour and salt. Add the eggs and flour alternately to the creamed mixture, beating well between each addition. Fold in the melted chocolate and add the milk and essence. Put into a greased 1½pt (900ml) pudding basin. Cover with greaseproof paper and foil and steam for 2 hours. Leave to stand in the basin for 5 minutes and turn on to a hot serving dish.

Helen's Pancake Layer
**

Pears with chocolate form a classic combination, commemorated in the ice-cream confection *Poire Belle Hélène*. This is a hot blend of the same flavours.

Ingredients
FOR 4–6

4oz (100g) plain flour
pinch of salt
1 egg
½pt (300ml) milk

FILLING

1½lb (675g) ripe pears
¼pt (150ml) water
1oz (25g) caster sugar
4oz (100g) plain chocolate
2 tbs lemon juice
2oz (50g) hazelnuts
vanilla ice cream
whipped cream

Prepare the pancakes first by mixing together the flour, salt, egg and milk to make a creamy batter. Fry 8 thin pancakes in lard or oil, and keep hot. While the pancakes are cooking, prepare the filling. Peel the pears and cut into neat slices. Put into a pan with the water and sugar and simmer until tender. Drain and keep the pears warm. In another bowl, melt the chocolate with the lemon juice over hot water. Chop the hazelnuts finely and stir into the chocolate.

Place a pancake on a warm serving dish, cover with pears and pour over a little chocolate sauce. Continue in layers, finishing with a pancake.

Serve at once cut in wedges, accompanied by scoops of vanilla ice cream and spoonfuls of whipped cream.

Hot Chocolate Soufflé
*

An impressive but easy soufflé, which you can partly prepare up to 8 hours beforehand.

Ingredients
FOR 4–6

4oz (100g) plain chocolate
2 tbs water
½pt (300ml) milk
1½oz (40g) butter
1½oz (40g) plain flour
¼ teasp vanilla essence
4 large eggs
2oz (50g) caster sugar
icing sugar

Put the chocolate into a pan with the water and 2 tbs milk. Stir over low heat until the chocolate has melted and add the remaining milk. Bring to the boil and remove from the heat. Melt the butter over low heat and stir in the flour. Cook over low heat for 1 minute. Remove from the heat and add the hot milk. Return to the heat and bring to the boil, stirring well until thick. Add the vanilla essence and leave until cool. Separate the eggs, and beat the yolks and sugar into the chocolate sauce. (At this point, the mixture may be left for up to 8 hours.)

Preheat the oven to 375°F/190°C/Gas 5 with a baking sheet inside placed in the centre of the oven. Grease a 2pt (900ml) soufflé dish well with butter and sprinkle with a little caster sugar. Whisk the egg whites to stiff but not dry peaks and fold into the chocolate mixture. Pour into the prepared dish, and run a spoon round the edge of the mixture (this makes the soufflé rise with a 'cauliflower' top). Place on the hot baking sheet and bake for 40 minutes.

Sprinkle with icing sugar and serve immediately with cream.

Steamed Chocolate Soufflé

A very rich but simple soufflé for those who are scared of making the traditional baked variety. Serve with *Chocolate Sauce (p109)* and/or cream.

Ingredients
FOR 6

8 medium slices white bread
6fl oz (175ml) double cream
5oz (125g) unsalted butter
7oz (200g) icing sugar
3½ oz (90g) ground almonds
4 eggs and 4 egg yolks
4oz (100g) plain chocolate
icing sugar

Grease a 2pt (1.2l) soufflé dish.

Discard the bread crusts and break the rest into crumbs. Pour on the cream and leave to soak. Break up the bread with a fork. Cream the butter and sugar until light and fluffy and then work in the almonds, eggs and egg yolks.

Break the chocolate into small pieces and melt in a bowl over a pan of hot water. Fold the chocolate into the mixture. Put into the soufflé dish and cover with greaseproof paper and foil. Steam for 2½ hours.

Sprinkle thickly with icing sugar and serve at once.

Little Chocolate Cream Soufflés

These individual soufflés are cooked until firm but still soft in the centre, and served with *Chocolate Sauce (p109)* or whipped cream.

Ingredients
FOR 6

4oz (100g) plain chocolate
¼pt (150ml) soured cream
few drops of vanilla essence
4 eggs
2oz (50g) caster sugar
icing sugar

Preheat the oven to 400°F/200°C/Gas 6. Grease 6 individual soufflé dishes very well with butter.

Break the chocolate into small pieces and put into a bowl over hot water. Heat gently until the chocolate has melted. Take off the heat and beat in the soured cream and vanilla essence.

Separate the eggs and beat the yolks into the chocolate one at a time. Whisk the egg whites to stiff peaks. Sprinkle in the caster sugar and continue beating until the mixture is shiny. Fold into the chocolate mixture until evenly coloured. Spoon into the dishes and place them on a baking sheet. Bake for 10 minutes. Sprinkle with icing sugar and serve at once.

6

COLD PUDDINGS

THE ADVANTAGE of a cold chocolate pudding is that it may be prepared well ahead of service. Indeed, a few hours' maturing can be a positive improvement, as flavours blend together to produce a smooth, subtle result. These cold puddings are perfect for special meals and buffet parties, and they should always be presented with flair on attractive dishes or in elegant bowls. Wine glasses make excellent receptacles for individual helpings, whether tall *flutes* or old-fashioned champagne *coupes*, placed on pretty plates or saucers, which can also hold the accompanying biscuit and spoon.

Over-decoration must be avoided with cold puddings, as a mass of piped cream and sprinkled decorations looks amateur and unappetising. Chocolate is so beautiful that it must be allowed to speak for itself, perhaps with the aid of some simple chocolate curls or other fancy bits (*see p121*). Whipped or pouring cream or an appropriate sauce may be handed separately. If a dish, such as a terrine, is obviously to be served in even-sized slices, these pieces may be presented on individual dishes in a shallow pool of sauce, perhaps decorated with a thin trail of cream, soft fruit or mint leaves.

Chocolate Rumpots
★

These chocolate pots should be made in very small dishes as the mixture is wonderfully rich. Serve them with pouring cream if you like.

Ingredients
FOR 4–6

7oz (200g) plain chocolate
½pt (300ml) single cream
1 egg
1 tbs rum

Grate 1oz (25g) chocolate coarsely. Break the remaining chocolate into small pieces and put into a heavy-based pan with the cream. Heat very gently until the chocolate has melted, and bring quickly to the boil. Whisk the egg with the rum. Take the pan off the heat and beat in the egg and rum mixture. Pour into 4–6 ramekin dishes and chill in the refrigerator for 24 hours. Sprinkle with grated chocolate before serving.

Double Chocolate Fudge Flan

★★

A sugary biscuit crust encloses a chocolate nut fudge filling, topped with soft chocolate.

Ingredients
For 6–8

4oz (100g) digestive biscuits
2oz (50g) unsalted butter
1oz (25g) demerara sugar

FILLING

10oz (300g) light soft brown sugar
¼pt (150ml) water
2oz (50g) unsalted butter
2oz (50g) plain chocolate
¼pt (150ml) double cream

TOPPING

4oz (100g) plain chocolate
1oz (25g) unsalted butter
grated plain chocolate

Crush the biscuits into crumbs. Melt the butter, remove from heat and stir in the crumbs and demerara sugar. Mix well and press into a greased 8in (20cm) flan ring placed on a serving dish.

Put the brown sugar and water into a heavy-based pan and heat gently until the sugar has dissolved. Boil for 1 minute and then simmer without stirring until the mixture is a pale fudge colour. Take off the heat and stir in the butter and chocolate broken into small pieces. Stir in the cream and bring slowly to the boil, then simmer for about 8 minutes until thickened.

Leave to cool for 10 minutes, stir well and pour into biscuit base. Put into the refrigerator for 20 minutes.

Break the chocolate into a bowl over a pan of hot water. Heat gently until melted.

Remove from heat and stir in the butter. Spread over the filling. Sprinkle thickly with grated chocolate and chill for 2 hours before serving with whipped or pouring cream.

Chocolate Mousse Cake

★★★

A rich ending to a simple meal, this flour-free 'cake' is sandwiched with chocolate cream.

Ingredients
For 6–8

9oz (250g) plain chocolate
1 teasp coffee powder
2 tbs brandy
2 tbs water
4 eggs
few drops of vanilla essence
2oz (50g) caster sugar
2 teasp cornflour
1oz (25g) cocoa powder

FILLING

¼pt (150ml) double cream
4oz (100g) plain chocolate
cocoa powder

Preheat the oven to 350°F/180°C/Gas 4. Lightly oil a 2lb (900g) loaf tin, and line the base and sides with baking parchment.

Break the chocolate into small pieces and put into a bowl with the coffee powder, brandy and water. Put over a pan of hot water and heat gently until the chocolate has melted. Remove from the heat, stir well and leave to cool.

Whisk the eggs, vanilla essence, sugar and cornflour until very thick, pale and creamy. Fold in the chocolate and cocoa powder. Put into the tin and bake for 1 hour. Leave in the tin for 5 minutes, then turn on to a piece of baking parchment on a wire rack to cool.

While the cake is cooling, prepare the filling. Put the cream into a small, heavy-based pan and bring to the boil. Break the chocolate into small pieces. Remove the cream from the heat and stir in the chocolate until melted. Return to the heat and bring to the boil again. Remove from the heat and cool. Slice the cake into four layers and sandwich together again with two-thirds of the cream mixture. Spread the remaining cream over the top and sides of the cake. Chill in the refrigerator for 20 minutes. Sprinkle with cocoa powder just before serving. The cake may be stored in the refrigerator for up to 4 days.

Chocolate Pavement
*

A French delicacy which is often served at Easter. You can vary the flavouring by using coffee powder or a little rum or liqueur instead of the orange rind.

Ingredients
FOR 6

10oz (300g) plain chocolate
6oz (175g) unsalted butter
4 egg yolks
2 teasp grated orange rind
10oz (300g) sponge fingers

Break the chocolate into small pieces and put into a bowl over a pan of hot water. Heat gently until melted and add the butter in small pieces. Stir well and remove from heat. Beat in the egg yolks, and stir in orange rind.

Count the sponge fingers and divide into three portions. Place one portion in a single layer on a serving dish. Cover with one-third of the chocolate mixture. Add a second portion of sponge fingers and a second portion of chocolate. Top with the remaining sponge fingers and spread the remaining chocolate mixture over the top and sides. Place in a refrigerator for 12 hours.

Chocolate Fruit Brulée
*

A wondrous blend of creamy chocolate with the sharpness of raspberries and crunchy caramel.

Ingredients
FOR 6

4oz (100g) raspberries
2 teasp kirsch
3 teasp caster sugar
3 egg yolks
1 teasp cornflour
½pt (300ml) single cream
4oz (100g) plain chocolate
6 teasp icing sugar

Take 6 individual ramekins and divide the raspberries between them. Sprinkle the fruit with kirsch and 1 teaspoon caster sugar. Put the remaining sugar into a bowl with the egg yolks and cornflour and mix well. Heat the cream gently to boiling point and pour into the bowl. Whisk well and return to the pan. Heat gently, stirring well until the mixture has thickened. Take off the heat and add the chocolate broken into small pieces. Stir until the chocolate has melted. Pour over the raspberries and chill in the refrigerator for 4 hours.

Place the ramekins on a baking sheet and sprinkle with icing sugar. Preheat a grill, and place the ramekins close to the grill until bubbles of dark caramel form. Cool for 30 minutes and serve.

Little Chocolate Custards

*

An Edwardian recipe with a delicate chocolate flavour which is not too rich at the end of a meal. For children, water may be used instead of brandy.

Ingredients
For 4–6

2oz (50g) plain chocolate
1pt (600ml) milk
2oz (50g) caster sugar
4 eggs
3 tbs brandy

Break the chocolate into small pieces and put into a heavy-based pan with the milk. Heat gently until the chocolate has melted. Whisk the sugar and eggs together and pour on the hot milk. Mix well and stir over low heat until the custard is thick and creamy. Remove from heat and cool to lukewarm. Stir in the brandy and pour into 4–6 individual glasses. If liked, serve with pouring cream.

Délice au Chocolat

*

The very best plain chocolate should be used for this recipe, which may be prepared at least 24 hours before being served.

Ingredients
For 8

4oz (100g) seedless raisins
4 tbs brandy
12oz (350g) plain chocolate
3 tbs strong coffee
6 eggs and 2 egg whites
10oz (300g) unsalted butter

Line a 9in (22.5cm) round cake tin with foil and brush lightly with oil. Soak the raisins in the brandy for 1 hour. Break the chocolate into small pieces and put into a bowl over a pan of hot water. Add the coffee and heat gently until melted. Take off the heat.

Separate the eggs and beat the yolks into the chocolate. Cream the butter until light and soft and gradually beat into the chocolate mixture. Whisk the egg whites to stiff peaks. Stir the raisins and brandy into the chocolate and then fold in the egg whites. Put into the prepared tin, cover with foil and chill in the refrigerator for 24 hours.

Turn on to a serving dish and mark the surface with patterns with a fork.

Chilled Chocolate Soufflé

**

A classic chocolate cream soufflé, standing high above the dish and decorated with cream and dark chocolate.

Ingredients
FOR 4–6

¾pt (450ml) milk
1½oz (40g) cocoa powder
3 eggs
3oz (75g) caster sugar
½pt (300ml) double cream
½oz (15g) gelatine
4 tbs water
2oz (50g) plain chocolate

Take a 1pt (600ml) soufflé dish and tie round it a double band of greaseproof paper to stand at least 2in (5cm) above the rim. Grease the dish and paper lightly. Put the milk and cocoa into a pan and bring to the boil, stirring well. Separate the eggs. Beat the sugar and egg yolks together in a bowl and stir in the milk. Return to the pan and heat gently, stirring all the time until the custard thickens. Cool to lukewarm. Whip half the cream and stir into the custard. Put the gelatine and water into a cup and stand it in a pan of hot water. Stir the gelatine until syrupy. Cool to the same temperture as the custard and stir it into the chocolate mixture. When it is just beginning to set, whisk the egg whites to soft peaks and fold into the mixture. Pour into the prepared dish and leave until set.

Carefully peel off the paper band. Whip the remaining cream and spread half of it round the edge of the soufflé. Grate the chocolate coarsely and press round the cream-covered sides, covering the cream completely. Pipe the remaining cream in rosettes on top of the soufflé.

Chocolate Roulade

**

A spectacular, delicious pudding which is easy to make. It must be made in advance, which is convenient for a dinner party.

Ingredients
FOR 6

6oz (175g) plain chocolate
5 eggs
6oz (175g) caster sugar
2 tbs hot water
½pt (300ml) double cream
icing sugar

Preheat the oven to 350°F/180°C/Gas 4. Oil a shallow 12x10in (30x25cm) tin and line with greaseproof paper.

Break the chocolate into small pieces and put into a bowl over a pan of hot water. Heat gently until melted. Separate the eggs and add the sugar to the yolks. Whisk until thick and pale. Cool the chocolate slightly and stir into the egg mixture. Stir in the hot water. Whisk the egg whites to stiff peaks and fold into the chocolate. Spread the mixture in the prepared tin and bake for 20 minutes. Cover with a piece of greaseproof paper and a cloth and leave overnight.

Put a piece of greaseproof paper on a flat surface and dust lightly with sieved icing sugar. Turn out the chocolate cake and remove paper. Whip the cream to soft peaks and spread lightly but evenly over the surface. Roll up like a Swiss roll (the surface may crack a little). Chill for 3 hours, and dust with sieved icing sugar.

Chocolate Hazelnut Gâteau

***

Nut meringue discs, layered with rich chocolate filling, for a gâteau which may be prepared the day before it is to be eaten.

Ingredients
FOR 8

2oz (50g) hazelnuts
4 egg whites
8oz (225g) light soft brown sugar
6oz (175g) unsalted butter
6oz (175g) granulated sugar
¼pt (150ml) water
3 egg yolks
4 oz (100g) plain chocolate
icing sugar

Spread the hazelnuts on a baking sheet and toast under a hot grill for a few minutes until the skins can be easily rubbed off in a cloth. Keep 12 nuts on one side and grind the rest in a blender.

Cover two baking sheets with parchment and mark two 6in (15cm) circles on each piece of baking parchment. Whisk the egg whites to stiff peaks and whisk in the sugar gradually until the mixture is stiff and shiny. Fold in the ground hazelnuts. Spread the mixture over the four circles. Bake at 275°F/140°C/Gas 1 for 1½ hours. Cool on the baking sheets and peel off the baking parchment.

To make the filling, soften the butter and beat until light and creamy. Put the sugar and water into a heavy-based pan and heat gently until the sugar has dissolved. Boil rapidly without stirring for about 10 minutes until the syrup will form long threads. Beat the egg yolks into a bowl and gradually pour the syrup over them, beating all the time (see Cook's Tip, p22). Blend in the butter and whip to a soft cream. Break the chocolate into small pieces and put into a bowl over hot water. When just melted, stir well and add to the buttercream. Leave in a cold place (for about 5 hours) until thick.

Sandwich together the meringue discs with the chocolate cream, saving enough for decoration. Sprinkle icing sugar over the surface. Put the remaining buttercream into a piping bag with a star nozzle and pipe a ring of stars all round the top edge of the cake. Arrange the reserved hazelnuts on the piped stars. Keep in a cold place before serving.

COOK'S TIP

If liked, a little coffee essence or rum may be added to the chocolate cream.

Mocha Icebox Cake

*

A very rich and delicious pudding, which requires no cooking.

Ingredients
FOR 4

5oz (125g) plain chocolate
5oz (125g) unsalted butter
5oz (125g) caster sugar
2 egg yolks
24 sponge finger biscuits
4fl oz (100ml) very strong black coffee
½pt (300ml) whipping cream

Put the chocolate into a small bowl and melt over hot water. Cream the butter and sugar until light and fluffy and work in the melted chocolate and the egg yolks. Dip 8 sponge fingers in coffee and arrange next to each other on a flat dish. Spread on one-third of the chocolate mixture. Dip 8 sponge fingers in the coffee and arrange on top with the biscuits facing the other way. Cover with one-third of the chocolate mixture. Dip the remaining sponge fingers in coffee and arrange on top in the same way as the first layer. Top with the remaining mixture. Cover loosely with foil and chill in the refrigerator for at least 6 hours. Whip the cream to soft peaks and cover the pudding just before serving.

Chocolate Chestnut Loaf

A very rich pudding which is most easily made with canned chestnut purée. Serve it in thin slices with whipped cream.

Ingredients
For 8

1lb (450g) unsweetened chestnut purée
6oz (175g) unsalted butter
4oz (100g) caster sugar
8oz (225g) plain chocolate
1 tbs brandy or coffee liqueur

Grease and line a 2lb (900g) loaf tin. Put the chestnut purée into a bowl. Soften the butter slightly and add to the purée with the sugar. Beat well until creamy and smooth. Break the chocolate into pieces and put into a bowl over a pan of hot water. Heat gently until just melted. Stir into the creamed mixture until evenly coloured and add the brandy or coffee liqueur. Put into the prepared tin and

smooth the surface. Chill in the refrigerator for 8 hours. Turn on to a serving dish and serve at once.

Chocolate Cream Sophie

A pudding which is wildly popular with chocolate addicts, but which is little more than an assembly job. The ingredients may be multiplied easily and it makes a cheap but effective pudding for large numbers.

Ingredients
For 6

4oz (100g) fresh brown breadcrumbs
4oz (100g) demerara sugar
8 teasp cocoa powder
4 teasp instant coffee powder
½pt (300ml) double cream
¼pt (150ml) single cream
grated plain chocolate (optional)

Stir together the breadcrumbs, sugar, cocoa powder and coffee powder until evenly coloured. Put the creams into a bowl and whip to soft peaks (it is most important that the cream is not whipped too stiffly or it will be impossible to assemble the pudding neatly).

Arrange in layers in a glass bowl, starting with crumbs and finishing with cream, and using three layers of crumbs and three layers of cream. Cover with foil and leave in the refrigerator for at least 4 hours before serving. If liked, sprinkle the surface with some grated plain chocolate at the last minute.

Julia's Chocolate Dinner Cake

**

A soft-textured, light, nutty pudding-cake. Serve it freshly baked with a bowl of sweetened whipped cream.

Ingredients

FOR 6–8

6oz (175g) unsalted butter
6oz (175g) caster sugar
3oz (75g) plain chocolate
4 eggs
4oz (100g) walnut kernels
3oz (75g) fine white breadcrumbs

TOPPING

4 tbs apricot jam
3oz (75g) plain chocolate
1½ oz (40g) unsalted butter

Preheat the oven to 475°F/240°C/Gas 9. Grease and base-line a 9in (22.5cm) round cake tin. Put the butter, sugar and chocolate into a bowl over hot water and heat until the chocolate has melted. Stir well together and leave until cool. Separate the eggs and beat in the egg yolks, one at a time. Grind the walnuts in a blender or food processor, and mix with the breadcrumbs. Whisk the egg whites to stiff peaks. Fold the crumb mixture and egg whites alternately into the chocolate. Put into the tin and place in the oven. Reduce the heat to 350°F/180°C/Gas 4 at once, and bake the cake for 50 minutes. Cool in the tin for 5 minutes and turn on to a wire rack to cool.

Lift on to a serving dish and spread the surface with apricot jam. Melt the chocolate and butter together in a bowl over hot water. Pour over the cake and leave until cold.

Wicked Chocolate Roll

**

Unspeakably rich and totally delicious, this pudding makes a spectacular finish to a dinner party, but needs a little last-minute attention. The faint-hearted may simply pour over the chocolate and cream and keep the cake flat, serving it in squares.

Ingredients

FOR 6–8

6 large eggs
8oz (225g) caster sugar
2oz (50g) cocoa powder
12oz (350g) plain chocolate
3 tbs water or black coffee
¾pt (450ml) double cream

Preheat the oven to 350°F/180°C/Gas 4. Grease and base-line a 12x8in (30x20cm) shallow tin. Separate the eggs and whisk the yolks until thick. Add the sugar and continue whisking until thick and pale lemon-coloured. Fold in the cocoa. Whisk the egg whites until stiff but not dry, and fold into the mixture. Spread lightly in the tin. Bake for 20 minutes until set but still slightly moist. Leave in the tin until cool and then turn on to a clean sheet of greaseproof paper on a flat dish. Melt the chocolate with the water or black coffee on a bowl over hot water. Cool but keep liquid. Whip the cream.

Just before serving, pour the chocolate over the cake and top with cream. Roll up quickly and serve at once – the soft chocolate and cream will ooze from the sides, but will look very enticing.

Mocha Charlotte

★★

This sumptuous pudding needs a little time to prepare, but the result is absolutely delicious.

Ingredients
For 6–8

4oz (100g) soft margarine
4oz (100g) caster sugar
4oz (100g) self-raising flour
1 tbs cocoa powder
2 eggs
1 tbs milk

FILLING

9oz (250g) plain chocolate
5 tbs strong black coffee
6 egg whites
3oz (75g) caster sugar

ASSEMBLY

½pt (300ml) strong black coffee
18–24 sponge fingers
plain chocolate
icing sugar

Preheat the oven to 350°F/180°C/Gas 4. Grease and base-line a 7in (17.5cm) round cake tin. Put the margarine, sugar, flour, cocoa powder, eggs and milk into a bowl and beat hard until light and creamy. Put into the prepared tin and bake for 35 minutes. Turn out and cool on a wire rack.

Break the chocolate into a heavy-based pan and add the coffee. Heat gently until the chocolate has melted. Remove from heat and leave to cool. Whisk the egg whites to stiff peaks and fold in the sugar. Add a little of the mixture to the chocolate and then gradually fold in all the egg mixture until the mousse is smooth and evenly coloured.

Take a 7in (17.5cm) cake tin and remove the base. Stand the metal ring on a serving plate. Split the chocolate cake into three layers. Put one layer on the plate and sprinkle with coffee. Carefully put the sponge fingers in a wall round the inside of the tin and outside the sponge base. Spoon in one-third of the chocolate mousse mixture. Cover with a second piece of sponge and sprinkle with coffee. Top with one-half of the remaining mousse, then with remaining sponge. Sprinkle with coffee and spoon in the remaining mousse. Grate some plain chocolate coarsely and sprinkle thickly on the surface. Refrigerate for 3 hours. Sprinkle with a light dusting of icing sugar. Carefully remove the cake tin just before serving.

Mocha Rum Creams

★

A wonderful balance of chocolate and complementary flavourings combine in this easy recipe. The slight sharpness of yoghurt offsets the richness of chocolate and cream, spiced with a hint of coffee and mellowed by rum and brown sugar.

Ingredients
For 6–8

½pt (300ml) whipping cream
½pt (300ml) natural yoghurt
3oz (75g) plain chocolate
3 tbs water
1 tbs instant coffee powder
2 tbs rum
2 tbs dark soft brown sugar

Whip the cream to soft peaks and fold in the yoghurt.

Put the chocolate, water and coffee powder into a bowl over a pan of hot water. When the chocolate has melted, remove from the heat and stir in the rum and sugar. Leave until cool and fold into the cream. Spoon into 6–8 individual pots and chill before serving.

Devil's Mountain
**

A mound of soft rum-soaked chocolate cake covered with cream and chocolate curls. It must be prepared 24 hours before serving.

Ingredients
For 6–8

5oz (125g) plain flour
1oz (25g) cocoa powder
2 teasp baking powder
pinch of salt
5oz (125g) light soft brown sugar
6 tbs corn oil
6 tbs milk
2 eggs

SYRUP

4oz (100g) granulated sugar
¼pt (150ml) water
4 tbs rum

COVERING

½pt (300ml) whipping cream
3oz (75g) plain chocolate

Preheat the oven to 350°F/180°C/Gas 4. Grease a 2pt (1.2l) pudding basin. Sieve the flour, cocoa powder, baking powder and salt into a bowl. Stir in the sugar until evenly coloured. Mix together the oil and milk. Separate the eggs and beat the yolks into the oil. Add to the dry ingredients and beat hard to a smooth batter. Whisk the egg whites to stiff peaks and fold into the mixture. Spoon into the basin and bake for 55 minutes until well-risen. Turn on to a wire rack to cool.

To make the syrup, put the sugar and water into a heavy-based pan and heat gently until the sugar has dissolved. Simmer for 5 minutes. Take off the heat and stir in the rum. Return the cold cake to the basin and prick all over the surface with a skewer. Pour over the hot syrup, cover and leave overnight. Just before serving, carefully turn the cake on to a serving dish. Whip the cream to soft peaks and spoon over the cake to cover it completely. Using a potato peeler, peel long curls of chocolate and sprinkle over the cake.

Chocolate Syllabub
*

In this mouthwatering modern version of a seventeenth-century dish, chocolate takes the place of the original fruit juices.

Ingredients
For 6

7 tbs boiling water
1 tbs cocoa powder
2oz (50g) caster sugar
2 tbs orange liqueur
½pt (300ml) double cream

Mix the water and cocoa and leave until cold. Add the sugar, liqueur and cream and whisk to soft peaks (the mixture splashes a lot, so use a large bowl). Pile into 6 glasses and chill before serving with sponge fingers or small sweet biscuits.

Profiteroles
★★

Little puffs of choux pastry are filled with cream and topped with *Chocolate Sauce* (*p109*). As a sumptuous alternative, fill the puffs with vanilla or coffee ice cream instead of whipped cream.

Ingredients
FOR 6

2oz (50g) butter
¼pt (150ml) water
2½oz (65g) plain flour
pinch of salt
2 eggs
½pt (300ml) double cream

Preheat the oven to 425°F/220°C/Gas 7. Rinse two baking sheets in cold water and leave wet (do not grease). Put the butter into a heavy-based pan. Add the water and bring to the boil. Sieve the flour and salt and tip into the liquid. Beat hard over low heat until the mixture is smooth and leaves the sides of the pan.

Remove from the heat and cool for 5 minutes. Add the eggs gradually, beating hard until the mixture is smooth and glossy. Make sure the baking sheets are still wet, and either pipe or spoon out with a teaspoon 18 small balls on to them, leaving plenty of room between them. Bake for 20 minutes without opening the oven. Take out of the oven and slit each bun with a sharp knife along one side. Leave until cold. Just before serving, fill with whipped cream or ice cream and pile in a pyramid on a serving dish. Serve with hot Chocolate Sauce.

Hungarian Mocha Gâteau
★★

This very special cake with a truffle filling and rich, fudge-like icing is best served after a simple meal.

Ingredients
FOR 8–10

3oz (75g) plain chocolate
6oz (175g) unsalted butter
4oz (100g) caster sugar
4 eggs
4oz (100g) plain flour
pinch of salt
1 teasp vanilla essence

FILLING

10oz (300g) plain chocolate
¾pt (450ml) whipping cream
2 tbs Tia Maria

ICING

4oz (100g) sugar
7 tbs strong black coffee
6oz (175g) plain chocolate
2 tbs golden syrup
1oz (25g) unsalted butter
2 tbs Tia Maria

Preheat the oven to 375°F/190°C/Gas 5. Grease and base-line two 9in (22.5cm) sponge sandwich tins. Put the chocolate into a bowl over a pan of hot water and heat until melted. Take off the heat and stir in the butter and sugar. Separate the eggs and stir the yolks into the chocolate mixture. Whisk the egg whites to stiff peaks and fold into the mixture. Sieve the flour and salt and fold into the chocolate, with the essence. Spoon into the prepared tins and bake for about 25 minutes until firm. Turn on to a wire rack to cool.

Make the filling by melting half the chocolate in a bowl over hot water. Whisk in the cream to make a light cream. Grate the remaining chocolate. Remove the cream mixture from the heat and stir in the grated chocolate and liqueur.

Put one of the cakes on a serving dish and spoon on the cream filling. Chill for 1 hour.

Make the icing by mixing the sugar with hot coffee and then boiling until a little of the mixture dropped into a cup of cold water forms a soft ball. Remove from the heat. Melt the chocolate in a bowl over hot water, cool and then stir in the coffee syrup. Add the golden syrup, butter and Tia Maria. Mix very well and pour over the top of the second cake. Leave until completely cold and firm and then place this cake layer on top of the chocolate cream. Chill for 1 hour before serving.

Fudge Pots
*

Little pots of soft chocolate fudge are wonderful served with whipped cream.

Ingredients
FOR 6

8oz (225g) plain chocolate
4 eggs
4oz (100g) unsalted butter
2 teasp caster sugar

Break the chocolate into small pieces and put into a bowl over hot water. Heat gently until melted. Separate the eggs and beat the yolks into the hot chocolate. Cut the butter into small pieces and add gradually to the chocolate, stirring well until

evenly blended. Remove from the heat and cool for 6 minutes. Whisk the egg whites to stiff peaks and whisk in the sugar. Fold into the chocolate mixture until evenly coloured. Divide among 6 individual ramekins or glasses. Chill for 24 hours. Serve with whipped cream.

Chocolate Truffle
**

This blissful pudding, much loved by chocolate fans, needs a little care when preparing the chocolate cream mixture.

Ingredients
FOR 8–10

4oz (100g) soft margarine
4oz (100g) caster sugar
4oz (100g) self-raising flour
1oz (25g) cocoa powder
2 eggs
1 tbs milk

SYRUP

2oz (50g) caster sugar
4 tbs water
2 tbs rum or orange liqueur

CHOCOLATE CREAM

¾pt (450ml) whipping cream
12oz (350g) plain chocolate
cocoa powder

Preheat the oven to 350°F/180°C/Gas 4. Grease and base-line a 9in (22.5cm) round cake tin.

Put the margarine, sugar, flour, cocoa powder, eggs and milk into a bowl and beat hard until light and creamy. Put into the prepared tin and bake for 25–30 minutes until firm. Turn on to a wire rack to cool. Prepare the syrup by putting the sugar and water into a small, heavy-based pan and heating gently until melted. Boil for 2 minutes, take off heat and stir in the rum or orange liqueur.

Place the cake on a serving dish. Cool the syrup and sprinkle all over the cake.

Whip the cream to soft peaks. Melt the chocolate in a bowl over hot water. Cool until still running easily but not hot. Pour on to the cream, mixing well until evenly coloured. Spoon over the cake. Refrigerate for 2–3 hours and sprinkle well with cocoa powder.

COOK'S TIP
FOR CHOCOLATE CREAM

Watch the temperature of the chocolate – if it is too hot it will cook and curdle the cream, but if it is too cool it will not blend easily into the cream. The texture should be like smooth whipped chocolate cream.

Chocolate Crackling Flan
★★

A crunchy flan case contrasts with a creamy chocolate filling and meringue topping.

Ingredients
For 6

6oz (175g) ground almonds
2oz (50g) caster sugar
1 teasp rum
1 egg white

FILLING AND TOPPING

8oz (225g) plain chocolate
8fl oz (225ml) double cream
1 egg yolk
1 tbs icing sugar
1 tbs rum
4 egg whites
4oz (100g) caster sugar
1oz (25g) flaked almonds

Butter an 8in (20cm) flan tin.

Stir together the almonds, sugar and rum until evenly coloured. Whisk the egg white to soft peaks and stir into the dry ingredients. Form into a ball, wrap in film and chill for 30 minutes. Preheat the oven to 350°F/180°C/Gas 4.

Roll out the dough on a lightly floured board and press into the prepared tin, patching the delicate dough if necessary. Cut a strip of foil to fit round the inside edge of the dough and press lightly to keep the dough firm. Bake for 25 minutes. Leave until cold and carefully remove the foil and the tin. Place the case on an ovenware serving plate.

To make the filling and topping, break the chocolate into small pieces and put into a bowl with the cream. Put over a pan of hot water and heat gently, stirring well until the mixture is smooth and thick. Take off the heat and leave to stand for 5 minutes. Stir in the egg yolk, icing sugar and rum and beat until light and fluffy. Pour into the flan case.

Whisk the egg whites to stiff peaks. Gradually beat in the sugar until firm and glossy. Spread over the chocolate filling to cover completely. Sprinkle with the flaked almonds. Bake at 450°F/230°C/Gas 8 for 5 minutes. Serve freshly baked.

Saint Emilion au Chocolate

*

St Emilion is known for its wine, but it is also the centre of a macaroon-baking industry. This local speciality combines chocolate with rum and the texture and flavour of almond macaroons.

Ingredients
FOR 6

12 almond macaroons
4 tbs rum
4oz (100g) unsalted butter
4oz (100g) caster sugar
¼pt (150ml) milk
1 egg
8oz (225g) plain chocolate

Put the macaroons in a single layer on a dish and sprinkle with the rum. Put the butter and sugar into a bowl and beat together until light and creamy. Bring the milk to the boil, take off the heat and leave to stand for 10 minutes before beating in the egg. Break the chocolate into small pieces and put into a bowl over a pan of hot water. Heat gently until the chocolate has melted and then leave over the heat while beating in the milk and the creamed butter mixture. Beat until very smooth.

Put 4 macaroons in the bottom of a serving bowl. Pour over half the chocolate mixture. Put 4 macaroons on top and cover with the remaining chocolate mixture. Top with the remaining macaroons. Cover with film and chill for 12 hours.

COOK'S TIP

Be sure to use real almond macaroons, not the cheaper coconut substitutes.

Floating Islands in a Chocolate Sea

**

A classic French pudding looks very dramatic when the sweet custard is replaced by a chocolate version,

Ingredients
FOR 4–6

6 eggs
13oz (375g) caster sugar
1pt (600ml) milk
2oz (50g) plain chocolate
cocoa powder or grated plain chocolate

Separate the eggs and whisk the whites to stiff peaks. Gradually add 9oz (250g) sugar to the egg whites, beating well between each addition. Put the milk and 2oz (50g) sugar into a heavy-based wide and shallow pan and bring just to boiling point. Using a tablespoon, take up a spoonful of the egg mixture and slide it gently on to the milk. Add more spoonfuls of egg mixture and poach for 3 minutes until firm, turning them once. Lift out with a slotted spoon and drain well. Continue until all the egg mixture has been used.

Strain the milk into a bowl. Whisk the egg yolks and remaining sugar until pale and creamy. Stir in the milk and put into a heavy-based pan. Heat gently, stirring well and gradually adding the broken chocolate. When the sauce coats the back of a spoon, pour into a glass bowl. Cool slightly and place poached meringues on the surface. Just before serving, sprinkle the meringues with cocoa powder or a little grated chocolate. Serve cold.

White Chocolate Terrine

**

A moulded white chocolate mousse which is particularly delicious served with fresh summer fruit such as strawberries or raspberries.

Ingredients
For 6

1 teasp gelatine
7 tbs water
2 tbs clear honey
10oz (300g) white chocolate
pinch of salt
3 egg yolks
12fl oz (350ml) whipping cream

Rinse a 1lb (450g) loaf tin in cold water and keep on one side. Put the gelatine and 2 tbs water into a cup and stand in a pan of hot water. Heat gently until the gelatine is syrupy. Put the honey into a heavy-based pan and add the remaining water. Bring to the boil and take off the heat. Break the chocolate into small pieces and stir into the honey. Add the gelatine and salt and stir until smooth. Stir in the egg yolks. Whip the cream to soft peaks and fold into the chocolate mixture. Spoon into the prepared tin and chill for 24 hours. Turn on to a serving dish and slice thickly to serve with fruit or with Chocolate Sauce (*p109*).

Chocolate Pavlova

**

Pavlova is an Australian version of meringue cake, with a crisp surface and marshmallow-like centre. Filled with chocolate cream, it is delicious served with fresh strawberries or raspberries.

Ingredients
For 6

3 egg whites
8oz (225g) caster sugar
1oz (25g) cocoa powder
1oz (25g) cornflour
1 teasp white vinegar
½pt (300ml) whipping cream
2oz (50g) plain chocolate
few drops of vanilla essence
8oz (225g) fresh strawberries or raspberries
icing sugar

Preheat the oven to 225°F/110°C/Gas ¼. Line a baking sheet with baking parchment and draw an 8in (20cm) circle in the centre.

Whisk the egg whites to stiff peaks and gradually whisk in half the sugar until stiff and glossy. Sieve the cocoa powder and cornflour together and fold into the meringue with the remaining sugar and the vinegar.

Spoon the meringue on to the circle and slightly scoop the centre of the meringue with the back of a spoon to form a slight well. Bake for 3 hours, turn off the oven and leave until cold. Carefully remove the meringue from baking parchment and place on a serving dish.

Just before serving, whip the cream to soft peaks. Grate the chocolate finely. Fold into the cream with the essence and spoon into the centre of the meringue. Top with a layer of fruit and sprinkle lightly with icing sugar.

Baked Chocolate Cheesecake

**

A creamy baked cheesecake on a nutty pastry base. Make it the day before serving so that the flavour matures.

Ingredients
FOR 6–8

2½oz (65g) plain flour
1oz (25g) ground hazelnuts or walnuts
1oz (25g) caster sugar
pinch of salt
1oz (25g) unsalted butter
2 teasp water

FILLING

1lb (450g) full fat soft cheese
5oz (125g) caster sugar
2 tbs plain flour
3 eggs
4oz (100g) plain chocolate
6 tbs double cream
grated plain chocolate and icing sugar

Stir together the flour, nuts, sugar and salt. Rub in the butter and add the water to make a dough. Gather into a ball, wrap in film and chill for 1 hour.

Preheat the oven to 400°F/200°C/Gas 6. Butter an 8 in (20cm) round cake tin with spring-form sides. Press the dough firmly into the base and bake for 15 minutes. Leave until cold.

To make the filling, beat the cheese until light and fluffy and work in the sugar and flour. Separate the eggs and beat in the yolks one at a time. Melt the chocolate in a bowl over hot water and gradually beat into the cheese mixture with the cream. Whisk the egg whites to soft peaks and fold into the chocolate.

Pour into the tin and bake at 325°F/160°C/Gas 3 for 1 hour. Turn off the oven and leave the cheesecake in for another 20 minutes. Remove from the oven and leave to stand until cold. Remove the sides of the tin, and place the cheesecake on a serving dish. Chill overnight. Sprinkle the surface thickly with grated plain chocolate and icing sugar.

Chilled Chocolate Cheesecake

**

A richly simple, gelatine-set cheesecake with a crunchy, chocolatey base.

Ingredients
FOR 8

1½oz (40g) butter
4oz (100g) plain chocolate digestive biscuits
2oz (50g) walnuts

FILLING

8oz (225g) full fat soft cheese
4oz (100g) caster sugar
1 tbs mint liqueur
4oz (100g) plain chocolate
½oz (15g) gelatine
8fl oz (225ml) water
¼pt (150ml) double cream
whipped cream, chocolate curls and walnuts

Preheat the oven to 350°F/180°C/Gas 4. Grease a 7in (17.5cm) cake tin with a removable base. Put the butter into a small pan and heat until melted. Crush the biscuits into crumbs and chop the walnuts finely. Stir into the butter and press on to the base of the prepared tin. Bake for 10 minutes. Leave until cold.

To make the filling, cream the cheese until smooth and gradually beat in the sugar and liqueur. Put the chocolate into a bowl over hot water and heat until melted. Gradually beat the chocolate into the cheese mixture. Put the gelatine and water into a cup and stand in a pan of hot water. Heat gently until the gelatine is syrupy and then beat into the cheese mixture. Whip the cream to soft peaks and fold into the mixture. Spoon over the biscuit base and chill until firm. Remove from the tin and decorate as liked with whipped cream, chocolate curls and walnut halves.

Chocolate Zabaglione

A classic Italian mixture of eggs, sugar and Marsala is flavoured with chocolate. Serve it freshly made and warm with sponge finger biscuits.

Ingredients
FOR 4

4 egg yolks
4oz (100g) caster sugar
4fl oz (100ml) Marsala
3 teasp cocoa powder

Put the egg yolks and sugar into a bowl over a pan of simmering water. Use a rotary or electric beater and whisk until thick and creamy. Gradually beat in the Marsala and cocoa powder, beating for about 5 minutes until the mixture is again thick and creamy and frothing well. Pour into 4 serving glasses and serve at once.

Mont Blanc

This very light chocolate sponge crowned with a peak of rum-flavoured cream looks and tastes spectacular.

Ingredients
FOR 6

8oz (225g) plain chocolate
2 tbs rum
1 tbs strong black coffee
4 oz (100g) unsalted butter
4 eggs
4oz (100g) caster sugar
3oz (75g) plain flour
1/2pt (300ml) double cream
1 tbs icing sugar

Preheat the oven to 350°F/180°C/Gas 4. Butter and lightly flour a Kugelhopf mould (if this is not available, use an ovenware pudding basin). Break the chocolate into small pieces and put into a bowl with half the rum and the coffee over a pan of hot water. Heat gently until the chocolate has melted. Take off the heat and add small pieces of butter, stirring until melted.

Separate the eggs and beat the yolks into the chocolate, one at a time. Stir in the sugar and flour until well mixed. Whisk the egg whites to stiff peaks and fold into the mixture. Pour into the prepared mould and bake for 45 minutes. Cool in the tin for 10 minutes and turn on to a serving dish.

Whip the cream and icing sugar to soft peaks and fold in the remaining rum. When the pudding is cold, spoon the cream into the centre and over the sides.

Chocolate Chestnut Gâteau

**

A cake with a mousse-like texture is layered with whipped cream and served with *Chocolate Sauce (p109)*.

Ingredients
FOR 6

4oz (100g) plain chocolate
4 eggs
7oz (200g) caster sugar
8oz (225g) unsweetened chestnut purée
pinch of salt
few drops of vanilla essence
½pt (300ml) double cream
cocoa powder
Chocolate Sauce

Preheat the oven to 350°F/180°F/Gas 4. Grease and base-line a Swiss-roll tin, approximately 12x9in (30x22.5cm).

Break the chocolate into small pieces and put into a bowl over a pan of hot water. Heat gently until melted. Whisk the eggs and sugar in a bowl over a pan of hot water until very pale and light. Whisk in the melted chocolate. Fold into the chestnut purée with the salt and essence. Spread in the prepared tin and bake for 20 minutes. Turn on to a piece of lightly sugared greaseproof paper to cool.

Cut the cake into three equal-sized rectangles and place one on a serving dish. Whip the cream to soft peaks and spoon half over the cake. Top with a second piece of cake, remaining cream and the remaining cake. Sprinkle lightly with cocoa powder. Serve at once with Chocolate Sauce.

Chocolate Mousse

*

This classic chocolate mousse may be flavoured with grated orange peel, rum, brandy or orange liqueur, and is best prepared the day before serving.

Ingredients
FOR 4–6

6oz (175g) plain chocolate
1 tbs water or black coffee
3 eggs
few drops of vanilla essence

Break the chocolate into small pieces and put into a bowl with water or coffee. Put over a pan of hot water and heat until the chocolate has melted. Separate the eggs and whisk the whites to stiff peaks. Remove the chocolate from the heat and cool for 5 minutes. Beat in the eggs and essence or any other flavouring. Fold in the egg whites until evenly coloured and pour into individual ramekins or glasses. Chill before serving with small sweet biscuits.

Mars Bar Mousse

*

A light-textured mousse with the magical flavour of Mars Bars and a toffee-like deposit at the base of each dish.

Ingredients
FOR 4–6

4oz (100g) Mars Bars
2oz (50g) plain chocolate
2 teasp water
3 eggs

Slice the Mars Bars thinly and put into a bowl with the broken chocolate and water. Put over a pan of hot water and heat gently until melted, stirring well. Separate the eggs and whisk the whites to stiff peaks. Remove the chocolate mixture from the heat and leave to cool for 6 minutes. Beat in the egg yolks and then fold in the egg whites. Divide between individual ramekins or glasses and chill before serving. Serve with cigarette biscuits or cat's tongues to dip into the toffee deposit.

Brandy Cream Mousse
★

This very rich mousse makes a perfect ending for a special party. You can also use crème de menthe or Grand Marnier instead of brandy, as exotic variations.

Ingredients
FOR 8

4oz (100g) plain chocolate
2 tbs water
5 eggs
2 tbs brandy
½pt (300ml) double cream
pinch of salt

Break the chocolate into pieces and put into a bowl with the water over a pan of hot but not boiling water. Separate the eggs and beat the yolks with the brandy. Beat into the chocolate and remove from the heat. Whip the cream to soft peaks and fold into the chocolate. Whisk the egg whites and salt to soft peaks and fold into the chocolate mixture. Spoon into 8 glasses. Chill for 12 hours before serving.

Double Chocolate Mousse
★★

Glasses of dark chocolate mousse laced with an orange liqueur are topped with a white chocolate mousse spiked with brandy, and the contrast is delicious.

Ingredients
FOR 8

12oz (350g) plain chocolate
6 tbs water
1oz (25g) unsalted butter
1 tbs orange-flavoured liqueur
6 eggs
12oz (350g) white chocolate
1 tbs brandy
grated plain chocolate

Break the plain chocolate into a bowl over a pan of hot water. Add 3 tbs of the water to the bowl. Heat gently until melted and then stir in the butter and orange-flavoured liqueur. Remove from the heat. Separate the eggs and beat 3 yolks into the chocolate. Whisk 3 egg whites to stiff peaks and fold into the mixture. Divide between 8 glasses and chill for 2 hours.

Break the white chocolate into a bowl and add the remaining 3 tbs of water. Put over a pan of hot water and heat gently until melted. Stir in the brandy and take off the heat. Beat in the remaining egg yolks. Whisk the remaining egg whites to stiff peaks and fold into the mixture. Pour over the dark mousse and chill until set. Sprinkle with grated chocolate and serve.

White Chocolate Mousse

**

Rum-flavoured white chocolate mousse to serve with a topping of grated plain chocolate or a few spoonfuls of *Chocolate Sauce (p109)*.

Ingredients
FOR 4–6

4oz (100g) white chocolate
2 tbs white rum
2 tbs water
¼pt (150ml) double cream
2 eggs
1 tbs milk
1 teasp gelatine
plain chocolate or Chocolate Sauce

Break the chocolate into small pieces and put into a bowl with the rum and water. Place over a bowl of hot water and heat until the chocolate has melted. Whip the cream to soft peaks. Separate the eggs and fold the yolks and chocolate into the cream. Put the milk into a cup and sprinkle in the gelatine. Stand the cup in a small pan of hot water and heat until the gelatine is syrupy. Stir into the chocolate mixture.

Cool until the mixture is beginning to set. Whisk the egg whites to stiff peaks and fold into the chocolate mixture. Spoon into individual ramekins and leave until set. Either sprinkle with grated chocolate or top with a spoonful of Chocolate Sauce.

7

ICES

A HOME-MADE ICE is the most delicious finish to a meal, and an even better refreshment between meals on a sunny morning or afternoon. Ices are not difficult to prepare, even with unsophisticated equipment. First-class ingredients are essential, carefully blended so that they withstand the freezing process. An emulsifying agent such as cream, custard, egg or gelatine gives smoothness; whisked egg whites give a light texture. Too much sweetening and too much alcohol inhibit freezing, so that mixtures of ingredients must be carefully balanced as in the following recipes.

Some recipes which are rich in emulsifying agents do not need beating during freezing, but others (such as sorbets) will need two or three beatings. This is most easily done by putting the half-frozen mixture into a food processor and blending until smooth before freezing again, and the process may be repeated two or three times. The ice may be frozen in a covered freezer box or metal container in the freezer or in the ice-making compartment of the refrigerator at lowest setting. All ices will taste better if taken from the freezer about twenty minutes before service, so that they soften slightly and the flavours recover from the intense cold.

For perfect ices, a *sorbetière* which freezes and churns is the answer, although expensive. A simpler version is a container which can be placed in the freezer and which has paddles which move constantly as the ice freezes. The result in both cases is a very smooth ice.

Like other cold puddings, an ice needs attractive presentation in a glass or metal container. A scoop dipped in hot water ensures beautifully domed portions, which may be arranged in containers and returned to the freezer before service (if the container is freezer-proof). A matching or contrasting sauce will make an ice a feast, and all sorts of flavoured ices, sauces and decorations may be combined to make attractive sundaes and *coupes*.

Chocolate Granita

An ice which has the texture of frozen snow, and which looks exciting served in tall glasses topped with whipped cream.

Ingredients
FOR 4

8oz (225g) sugar
½pt (300ml) water
4oz (100g) plain chocolate

Put the sugar and half the water into a heavy-based pan and heat gently until the sugar has dissolved. Bring to the boil without stirring and simmer for about 5 minutes to make a syrup. Add the remaining water and the chocolate broken into small pieces and stir until the chocolate has melted. Leave for 1½ hours until cold and pour into a freezing tray. Freeze to a firm mush, stirring once or twice. To serve, spoon into tall glasses and top with whipped cream.

White Chocolate Ice Cream

For those who like a sweet chocolate flavour, this ice cream is good served with *Dark Chocolate Rum Sauce (p111)* or *Raspberry Liqueur Sauce (p113)*.

Ingredients
FOR 6

½pt (300ml) single cream
4oz (100g) white chocolate
2oz (50g) caster sugar
6 egg yolks

Put the cream into a heavy-based pan with the chocolate and sugar. Heat gently until the chocolate has melted. Whisk the egg yolks in a bowl. Slowly pour on the chocolate and whisk until well blended. Return to the pan and heat gently until smooth and thick, but do not boil. Leave until cold and freeze for 3 hours, stirring twice during freezing.

Chocolate Rum Sorbet

For the smoothest texture, this sorbet is best made in an ice-cream machine, but it may be half-frozen and then whirled in a food processor to break up crystals.

Ingredients
FOR 6

1lb (450g) sugar
2pt (1.2l) water
8oz (225g) plain chocolate
2 teasp coffee powder
½ teasp ground cinnamon
pinch of salt
4 tbs rum

Put the sugar, water, broken chocolate, coffee powder, cinnamon and salt into a heavy-based pan. Bring slowly to the boil, stirring until the sugar has dissolved. Boil for about 5 minutes, stirring occasionally, to make a chocolate syrup. Remove from the heat and cool to lukewarm. Stir in the rum. Either freeze in an ice-cream machine, or put into the freezer for 1½ hours until half-frozen, before whirling with a food processor and then freezing until firm. Serve in scoops, with whipped cream if liked, and with small sweet biscuits.

Rum Bumble Ice
★★

Rich rum-flavoured ice cream filled with soft raisins and walnuts.

Ingredients
For 4-6

5 tbs rum
2oz (50g) seedless raisins
2oz (50g) walnuts
1¹/₂oz (40g) cocoa powder
2 tbs boiling water
3oz (75g) plain chocolate
4 eggs
4oz (100g) caster sugar
¹/₂pt (300ml) double cream

Put the rum into a bowl with the raisins. Chop the walnuts roughly and add to the bowl. Leave to stand for 1 hour. In another bowl, mix the cocoa powder and water and add the chocolate broken into small pieces. Put over a pan of hot water and heat gently until the chocolate has melted. Separate the eggs and stir the yolks together until well mixed. Whisk the egg whites to stiff peaks and gradually whisk in the sugar. Whip the cream to soft peaks. Work the chocolate mixture into the egg yolks and stir in the raisins, nuts and rum. Fold in the egg whites and the cream. Put into a covered container and freeze for 3–4 hours until firm. Before serving, leave at room temperature for 5–10 minutes.

Rum Parfait
★

A light, creamy ice spiked with rum and enhanced by *Chocolate Sauce (p109)*.

Ingredients
For 6

2oz (50g) caster sugar
4 tbs water
4oz (100g) plain chocolate
3 egg yolks
2 tbs rum
¹/₂pt (300ml) double cream
3 tbs Chocolate Sauce

Put the sugar and water into a small, heavy-based pan. Heat gently until the sugar has dissolved and then boil to make 4 tbs syrup. Break the chocolate into small pieces and place in a liquidiser. Pour in the hot syrup and blend enough to break up the chocolate. Add the yolks and rum and blend until smooth.

Whip the cream to soft peaks. Pour on the chocolate mixture and whisk until well mixed. Spoon into 6 individual ramekins. Place on a baking sheet, cover and freeze for 3 hours. To serve, remove from freezer and leave at room temperature for 5 minutes. Spoon Chocolate Sauce over each serving to cover the surface. Serve at once with small sweet biscuits.

Mocha Ice Cream

The unbeatable combination of chocolate and coffee makes a sophisticated ice cream. For added luxury, serve each portion with a spoonful of rum or Tia Maria.

Ingredients
For 6

4oz (100g) light soft brown sugar
2oz (50g) unsalted butter
2oz (50g) cocoa powder
1oz (25g) coffee powder
5 tbs water
¾pt (450ml) whipping cream

Put the sugar, butter, cocoa powder, coffee powder and water into a small, heavy-based pan. Heat gently, stirring until the butter has melted. Bring to the boil, remove from the heat and leave until cool. Whip the cream to soft peaks, and then gradually whisk in the chocolate mixture. Freeze for 1½ hours until half-frozen and then beat very well until smooth. Return to the freezer until firm. Allow 20 minutes out of the freezer before serving.

Double Chocolate Ice Cream

Creamy chocolate ice cream dotted with tiny chunks of plain chocolate. For the addict, serve it with *Chocolate Fudge Sauce (p112)* or *Mint Cream (p112)*.

Ingredients
For 6

8oz (225g) plain chocolate
½pt (300ml) milk
3 egg yolks
3oz (75g) caster sugar
½pt (300ml) double cream

Break half the chocolate into pieces and put into a heavy-based pan with the milk. Heat gently until the chocolate has melted, and stir until smooth. Whisk the egg yolks and sugar together until the mixture is very pale and thick. Gradually whisk in the chocolate milk. Return to the pan and cook very gently until the mixture thickens. Leave until cold, stirring occasionally. Whip the cream to soft peaks and fold into the chocolate custard.

Freeze for 1½ hours until half-frozen, and then beat well. Chop the remaining chocolate finely and fold into the ice cream. Continue freezing for 1½ hours, beating twice more.

Chocolate Fudge Ice Cream

★

A lightly flavoured chocolate ice cream given a special flavour and texture with small pieces of chocolate fudge. If possible use a good home-made fudge, such as one of the recipes on pp102–3.

Ingredients

FOR 6

4oz (100g) light soft brown sugar
¼pt (150ml) water
4 egg yolks
1 tbs cocoa powder
¾pt (450ml) double cream
8oz (225g) chocolate fudge

Put the sugar and water into a small, heavy-based pan. Heat gently until the sugar has dissolved, and then boil for 5 minutes. Whisk the egg yolks and cocoa powder together and gradually pour in the hot syrup, beating well all the time. Continue beating until cool. Whip the cream to soft peaks and fold in the egg mixture. Freeze for 1½ hours until half-frozen and then beat well until creamy. Continue freezing for 1 hour, beating once more.

Chop the fudge roughly. Beat the ice cream and fold in the fudge pieces. Continue freezing for 30 minutes. To serve, leave in the refrigerator for 15 minutes before scooping so that the fudge softens slightly.

Brown Bread Chocolate Ice Cream

★

Brown bread ice cream was a Victorian favourite and its unusual texture is enhanced by small pieces of chocolate. For added bliss, serve the ice cream with *Dark Chocolate Rum Sauce (p111)*.

Ingredients

FOR 6

½pt (300ml) double cream
¼pt (150ml) single cream
2 eggs
3oz (75g) icing sugar
3oz (75g) plain chocolate
4oz (100g) wholemeal bread

The breadcrumbs should not be too fine but should retain a crumbly texture. Put the double cream and single cream into a bowl and whip to soft peaks. Separate the eggs and beat the yolks and sugar until pale and thick. Chop the chocolate very finely. Mix the breadcrumbs and chocolate into the egg yolk mixture and fold into the whipped cream. Whisk the egg whites to stiff peaks and fold into the mixture. Freeze for 3 hours until firm.

Frozen Chocolate Soufflé

**

A spectacular-looking and very light ice, which may be served with a sauce (*pp109-13*) and small sweet biscuits.

Ingredients
FOR 6

3 eggs
2oz (50g) caster sugar
4oz (100g) plain chocolate
¾pt (450ml) double cream
plain chocolate and icing sugar

Prepare a 1pt (600ml) soufflé dish by tying a double piece of greaseproof paper round the dish to stand 2in (5cm) above the rim.

Separate the eggs and put the yolks and sugar into a bowl over a pan of hot water. Whisk until the sugar has dissolved and the mixture forms thick ribbons. Melt the chocolate in a bowl over hot water and then whisk into the egg mixture until cool. Whip the cream to soft peaks and fold into the chocolate mixture. Whisk the egg whites to stiff peaks and fold into the mixture until evenly coloured. Spoon into the prepared dish and freeze for 4 hours.

To serve, remove the paper. Grate some plain chocolate coarsely and sprinkle over the top surface, then dust lightly with icing sugar.

Peppermint Cream Ice

*

Chocolate and peppermint combine in an ice cream with a slightly crunchy texture. Serve each portion decorated with a thin peppermint cream.

Ingredients
FOR 6

4 egg yolks
6oz (175g) caster sugar
½pt (300ml) milk
4oz (100g) plain chocolate
2 tbs crème de menthe
3oz (75g) chocolate mint crisps
½pt (300ml) double cream

Whisk the egg yolks and sugar together until very pale and creamy. Heat the milk and chocolate in a heavy-based pan until just boiling. Gently pour on to the egg mixture, whisking all the time. Return to the pan and cook over gentle heat until thick and creamy. Remove from the heat and leave until cold. Stir in crème de menthe. Grate the chocolate mint crisps and fold into the chocolate mixture.

Whip the cream to soft peaks and fold into the chocolate custard. Freeze for 1½ hours until half-frozen. Beat well and return to the freezer for 1½ hours, beating once more during freezing.

Chocolate Roulade (p43)
White Chocolate Terrine (p53)
White Chocolate and Dark Chocolate
  Ice Creams (p60 & 67)
Coffee Truffle Bombe with
  Mocha Cream Sauce (p67)

Nutty Chocolate Terrine

*

A rich chocolate ice studded with three kinds of nuts and made in a loaf shape for easy slicing. Serve with *Crème Anglaise* (*p113*) or *Dark Chocolate Rum Sauce* (*p111*).

Ingredients
FOR 8

8oz (225g) caster sugar
6 egg yolks
8oz (225g) plain chocolate
1pt (600ml) whipping cream
3oz (75g) walnuts
3oz (75g) hazelnuts
3oz (75g) flaked almonds

Whisk the sugar and egg yolks together until very pale and creamy. Break the chocolate into small pieces and melt in a bowl over a pan of hot water. Cool slightly and fold into the whisked mixture. Whip the cream to soft peaks and fold into the chocolate. Chop the walnuts and hazelnuts and add all the nuts to the mixture. Line a 2lb (900g) loaf tin with foil and spoon in the mixture. Cover and freeze for 6 hours. To serve, leave to stand in the refrigerator for 30 minutes, turn out and peel off the foil. Cut into slices and place each serving on a pool of the chosen sauce.

Frozen Mocha Mousse

*

A very light iced mousse which may be prepared up to 10 days in advance.

Ingredients
FOR 6

4oz (100g) plain chocolate
1 tbs cocoa powder
1 teasp coffee powder
2 tbs boiling water
6 egg whites
3oz (75g) caster sugar
grated plain chocolate

Break the chocolate into pieces and put into a bowl over a pan of hot water. Heat gently until melted. Mix the cocoa powder, coffee powder and water to a paste and stir into the chocolate, mixing well until thick and creamy.

Whisk the egg whites to stiff peaks. Gradually add the sugar, whisking all the time until the mixture is glossy. Fold in the chocolate mixture until thoroughly blended. Spoon into 6 ramekins. Place on a metal tray, and cover with freezer film. Freeze for 2 hours until firm. Store in the freezer for up to 10 days. Serve frozen with a sprinkling of grated chocolate.

Chocolate Fruit Bombe

*

An impressive frozen pudding which may be made 24 hours before serving.

Ingredients
FOR 6

4oz (100g) plain chocolate
¾pt (450ml) double cream
1lb (450g) can apricots
2 tbs bitter orange marmalade
2 teasp brandy
grated plain chocolate

Brush a 1½pt (900ml) metal bowl with flavourless oil. Break the chocolate into small pieces and put into a bowl over hot water. Heat gently until melted. Remove from the heat. Whip the cream to soft peaks, and put one-third into another bowl. Stir the larger portion of cream into the chocolate. Line the prepared bowl with the chocolate mixture. Cover and freeze until firm.

Drain the apricots and put into a blender or food processor with the marmalade and brandy. Blend and pour the mixture into the chocolate case. Cover and freeze for 6 hours until firm. To serve, put into a refrigerator for 1 hour before turning out on to a serving plate. Decorate with the remaining whipped cream and sprinkle with grated chocolate.

Chocolate Brandy Terrine

**

A light chocolate ice layered with sweet prunes soaked in brandy, to be served with *Creme Anglaise (p113)* or *Chocolate Sauce (p109)*.

Ingredients
FOR 8

8oz (225g) large prunes
6 tbs brandy or Armagnac
6 eggs
4oz (100g) caster sugar
8oz (225g) plain chocolate
1pt (600ml) whipping cream

Cut the prunes in half and discard the stones. Put into a bowl and cover with the brandy or Armagnac. Leave to stand while preparing the ice cream.

Separate the eggs and whisk the yolks with the sugar until very pale and creamy. Break the chocolate into small pieces and melt in a bowl over a pan of hot water. Cool slightly and fold into the whisked mixture. Whisk the egg whites to stiff peaks. Whip the cream to soft peaks. Fold the egg whites and cream into the chocolate mixture. Drain the prunes and fold in any liquid.

Line a 2lb (900g) loaf tin with foil and spoon in half the mixture. Cover with the prunes and top with the remaining chocolate mixture. Cover and freeze for 6 hours.

To serve, leave to stand in the refrigerator for 30 minutes, turn out and peel off the foil. Cut into slices and serve with chosen sauce.

Coffee Truffle Bombe with Mocha Cream Sauce

★★

A rich coffee ice cream stuffed with chocolate truffles and served with a mocha cream sauce.

Ingredients
FOR 6–8

1 tbs coffee powder
1 tbs boiling water
3 eggs
4oz (100g) caster sugar
1pt (600ml) double cream
2 tbs coffee liqueur

TRUFFLE FILLING

4oz (100g) plain chocolate
2oz (50g) unsalted butter
2 tbs double cream
2 tbs icing sugar

SAUCE

4oz (100g) plain chocolate
¼pt (150ml) double cream
1 tbs coffee liqueur

Dissolve the coffee in boiling water and leave until cold. Whisk the eggs and sugar in a bowl over hot water until thick, white and creamy. Leave until cold. Whip the cream, coffee and liqueur to stiff peaks and fold in the egg mixture. Pour into a freezer tray, cover and freeze for 3 hours until firm.

While the ice cream is freezing, prepare the truffles. Melt the chocolate and butter together in a bowl over a pan of hot water. Remove from the heat and stir in the cream and icing sugar. Mix well and chill until firm. Roll into balls and refrigerate until the ice cream is ready.

Beat the ice cream with an electric mixer or food processor until soft and smooth. Put a layer of ice cream into a 2pt (1.2l) pudding basin and arrange some truffles on top. Add another layer of ice cream and remaining truffles, and top with ice cream. Cover and freeze for 3 hours until firm.

Just before serving, prepare the sauce. Melt the chocolate in a bowl over a pan of hot water. Remove from heat and stir in the cream and liqueur. Unmould the iced bombe on to a serving dish, and serve each portion with some of the sauce.

Dark Chocolate Ice Cream

★

A deeply flavoured ice which is delicious on its own, or used as a base for a sundae with sauce, nuts and whipped cream.

Ingredients
FOR 6

1pt (600ml) creamy milk
5oz (125g) caster sugar
4oz (100g) plain chocolate
3oz (75g) cocoa powder
½pt (300ml) double cream

Put the milk and sugar into a heavy-based pan and just bring to the boil. Take off the heat and add the chocolate broken into small pieces. Stir until well mixed. Whisk in the cocoa powder and return to heat for 2 minutes. Leave until cold, stirring occasionally. Whip the cream to soft peaks and fold in the chocolate mixture. Freeze for 1½ hours until half-frozen and beat well until smooth. Freeze again for 1 hour, beat again, and freeze until firm.

8
CAKES AND BISCUITS

ALL CHOCOHOLICS LOVE CHOCOLATE CAKE. There is never any doubt which will be the most popular cake on the table or biscuit in the tin, but there are dozens of ways of producing the most perfect confection. There is, of course, the simple chocolate sponge, layered with buttercream and topped with icing, or there may be the more sophisticated fudgy-chocolate cake filled with a slightly sharp fruit jam and covered with a soft chocolate glaze. There may be truffle cakes and meringues, chewy brownies and wicked combinations of shortbread, toffee and plain chocolate. There may be biscuits dipped in soft chocolate, or layered with coffee cream, and tray-baked squares dripping with chocolate icing. This chapter contains just about everyone's favourite chocolate cake or biscuit.

There is no magic in producing a good result, but there must be attention to detail. As with all chocolate cookery, it is important to use the best ingredients – nothing tired or stale, or cheap-tasting. It is then important to measure them accurately, and to combine them in the way described in a recipe. It is also important to use the correct sized tin for baking, or the area of the mixture will be altered, which can result in an undercooked or over-baked cake. Finally, it is important to set the oven at the correct temperature, and to be sure that it has reached that temperature before use. Many chocolate mixtures are fragile, and it is usually best to allow cakes to set in their tins for a few minutes before turning them out for final cooling. In other words, follow each recipe exactly for perfect results.

As with puddings, don't be tempted to over-decorate cakes. The rich chocolate finish speaks for itself, only needing a simple chocolate decoration to make it luxurious.

Chocolate Bran Cake

★

The bran gives a lovely texture to this simple cake, finished with orange-hinted chocolate icing.

Ingredients
MAKES 8IN (20CM) CAKE

1oz (25g) All Bran cereal
4 tbs milk
2oz (50g) butter
2oz (50g) dark soft brown sugar
1 egg
1¹/₂oz (40g) plain chocolate
2oz (50g) self-raising flour

ICING

2oz (50g) plain chocolate
1oz (25g) butter
1 tbs milk
2oz (50g) icing sugar
¹/₂ teasp grated orange rind

Preheat the oven to 350°F/180°C/Gas 4. Grease and base-line an 8in (20cm) round cake tin. Put the cereal and milk into a small bowl and leave until the milk has been absorbed. Cream the butter and sugar until light and fluffy. Beat the egg lightly. Melt the chocolate. Beat the cereal mixture, egg and flour into the creamed mixture and finally stir in the melted chocolate. Put into the tin and make a slight hollow in the surface. Bake for 40 minutes and turn on to a wire rack to cool.

To make the icing, put the chocolate, butter and milk into a bowl over a pan of hot water, and stir until the chocolate has melted. Take off the heat and gradually stir in the icing sugar and orange rind. The mixture should be a thick pouring consistency, but if not, leave to cool slightly before using. Pour over the cake and leave until cold.

Chocolate Ginger Cake

★

An unusual combination of chocolate and ginger, with a light gingerbread paired with whipped cream and a dark chocolate icing.

Ingredients
FOR AN 8IN (20CM) CAKE

6oz (175g) butter or soft margarine
5oz (125g) dark soft brown sugar
3 eggs
6oz (175g) self-raising flour
3 teasp ground ginger

FILLING

¹/₄pt (150ml) whipping cream

ICING

3oz (75g) plain chocolate
2 tbs water
1oz (25g) butter or margarine
8oz (225g) icing sugar
2oz (50g) crystallised ginger

Preheat the oven to 350°F/180°C/Gas 4. Grease and base-line two 8in (20cm) sandwich tins. Cream the fat and sugar until light and fluffy. Beat the eggs lightly. Sieve the flour and ginger together. Add eggs and flour alternately to the creamed mixture, beating well between each addition. Divide between the two tins and bake for 30 minutes. Turn on to a wire rack to cool.

Whip the cream to soft peaks and use to sandwich the cakes together. Put the chocolate, water and fat into a bowl over a pan of hot water and stir until the chocolate melts. Remove from the heat and beat in the sugar gradually. Spread over the top of the cake and decorate with the crystallised ginger.

Chocolate Parkin

The rich gingerbread which is tradition-ally eaten on Guy Fawkes' Day tastes very special when combined with chocolate.

Ingredients
FOR A 6IN (15CM) SQUARE CAKE

4oz (100g) butter
4oz (100g) black treacle
4oz (100g) dark soft brown sugar
½ teasp bicarbonate of soda
6 tbs milk
4oz (100g) plain flour
4oz (100g) fine oatmeal
1 teasp ground ginger
1 teasp ground mixed spice
pinch of salt
1 egg
4oz (100g) plain chocolate

Preheat the oven to 325°F/160°C/Gas 3. Grease and base-line a 6in (15cm) square cake tin. Put the butter, treacle and sugar into a pan and heat gently until the fat has melted. Leave to cool. Stir the bicarbonate of soda into the milk. Stir the flour, oatmeal, ginger, spice and salt together. Beat in the butter mixture, milk and egg. Chop the chocolate finely and stir into the cake mixture. Put into the prepared tin and bake for 1 hour. Cool in the tin for 5 minutes and turn on to a wire rack to finish cooling. Store in a tin for 3 days before using.

Chocolate Marble Cake

An old-fashioned nursery cake which is simple to make but looks spectacular.

Ingredients
FOR A 7IN (17.5CM) CAKE

8oz (225g) soft margarine
8oz (225g) caster sugar
few drops of vanilla essence
3 large eggs
10oz (300g) self-raising flour
3oz (75g) plain chocolate

Preheat the oven to 350°F/180°C/Gas 4. Grease and base-line a 7in (17.5cm) round cake tin. Cream the fat, sugar and essence until light and fluffy. Beat the eggs lightly together. Sieve the flour. Add the eggs and flour alternately to the creamed mixture.

Put half the mixture into another bowl. Melt the chocolate in a bowl over hot water and beat into half the mixture. Put alternate spoonfuls of plain and chocolate mixture into the prepared tin. Bake for 45 minutes. Cool in the tin for 2–3 minutes and turn on to a wire rack to cool.

Chocolate Caramel Cake

*

Everyone loves chocolate caramels, so it is worth combining the two distinctive flavours for a popular cake.

Ingredients

FOR A 7IN (17.5CM) CAKE

4oz (100g) soft margarine
4oz (100g) caster sugar
4oz (100g) self-raising flour
1oz (25g) cocoa powder
2 eggs
2 tbs milk

TOPPING

3oz (75g) sugar
2 tbs double cream
1 tbs plain flour
2oz (50g) whole blanched almonds
1oz (25g) grated plain chocolate

Preheat the oven to 375°F/190°C/Gas 5. Grease and base-line a 7in (17.5cm) round cake tin.

Put the margarine, sugar, flour, cocoa and eggs into a bowl with the milk and beat hard with a wooden spoon until light and soft. Put into the prepared tin and bake for 25 minutes.

Put the sugar in a small pan and heat gently until melted. Stir in the cream, flour and almonds. Pour over the cake and continue baking for 10 minutes. Leave in the tin for 2 minutes and turn on to a wire rack to cool, with caramel side upwards. After 10 minutes, sprinkle the surface with grated chocolate.

Chocolate Rum Cake

**

Chocolate and rum are natural partners, and they are combined here in a rich, dark cake for a special occasion.

Ingredients

FOR A 8IN (20CM) CAKE

6oz (175g) butter or soft margarine
6oz (175g) caster sugar
6 tbs black treacle
2 eggs
6oz (175g) self-raising flour
1oz (25g) cocoa powder
1oz (25g) cornflour
5 tbs milk

FILLING AND ICING

8oz (225g) unsalted butter
12oz (350g) icing sugar
2 tbs black treacle
6 tbs milk
2 tbs rum
4 tbs boiling water

Preheat the oven to 350°F/180°C/Gas 4. Grease and base-line two 8 in (20cm) sandwich tins.

Cream the fat, sugar and treacle until light and fluffy. Beat the eggs lightly. Sieve the flour, cocoa powder and cornflour together. Add to the creamed mixture alternately with the milk, and the eggs, beating well between each addition. Divide between the two tins and bake for 30 minutes. Turn on to a wire rack to cool. When cold, split each cake into two layers.

To make the icing, cream the butter, sugar and treacle together. Work in the milk and rum slowly and finally whisk in the boiling water, a little at a time. Sandwich the layers together and use any surplus icing for the top of the cake.

Rich Dark Chocolate Cake

★

The unusual addition of Guinness results in a chocolate cake which is very dark but light-textured.

Ingredients
FOR AN 8IN (20CM) CAKE

4oz (100g) soft margarine
6oz (175g) dark soft brown sugar
2 eggs
6oz (175g) plain flour
1 teasp baking powder
½ teasp bicarbonate of soda
¼pt (150ml) Guinness
2oz (50g) cocoa powder

FILLING AND ICING

4oz (100g) plain chocolate
1 tbs milk
4oz (100g) soft margarine
8oz (225g) icing sugar
walnut halves

Preheat the oven to 350°F/180°C/Gas 4. Grease and base-line two 8in (20cm) sandwich tins.

Cream the fat and sugar until light and fluffy. Beat the eggs lightly. Sieve the flour, baking powder and soda. Add the eggs and flour alternately to the creamed mixture, beating well between each addition. Mix the Guinness and cocoa powder together to make a thick paste. Stir into the cake mixture and beat just enough to mix. Divide between the tins and bake for 30 minutes. Cool on a wire rack.

To make the icing, put the chocolate and milk into a bowl over a pan of hot water. When the chocolate has melted, remove from the heat and cool to lukewarm. Cream the fat and sugar together and beat in the chocolate until evenly coloured. Use one-third of the icing to put the two cake halves together. Swirl the remaining icing on top and decorate with walnut halves.

Brazilian Chocolate Cake

★

Nuts, dates and cherries combine with chocolate chips in a cut-and-come-again cake which needs no decoration.

Ingredients
FOR A 2LB (900G) LOAF CAKE

4oz (100g) dates
8oz (225g) Brazil nuts
2oz (50g) glacé cherries
4oz (100g) chocolate chips
4oz (100g) plain flour
½ teasp baking powder
pinch of salt
5½oz (150g) sugar
3 eggs

Preheat the oven to 375°F/190°C/Gas 5. Grease and base-line a 2lb (900g) loaf tin.

Reserve 6 dates and 6 nuts and chop the rest roughly. Put into a bowl. Cut the cherries in half and add to the bowl with the chocolate chips. Sieve the flour, baking powder and salt and add to the bowl with the sugar. Stir well. Separate the eggs and whisk the whites until frothy. Stir in the yolks and add to the bowl. Mix well and put into the prepared tin. Arrange reserved dates and nuts on top. Bake for 1½ hours. Turn on to a wire rack to cool.

Chocolate Fudge Layer Cake

**

A dark, dense chocolate cake with creamy fudge filling and topping – lovely for tea, or as a pudding.

Ingredients

FOR AN 8IN (20CM) CAKE

4oz (100g) plain chocolate
3 tbs boiling water
7oz (200g) self-raising flour
1oz (25g) cocoa powder
6oz (175g) unsalted butter
6oz (175g) caster sugar
1 teasp vanilla essence
4 eggs
2 tbs milk

FILLING AND TOPPING

7oz (200g) plain chocolate
6fl oz (175ml) evaporated milk
8oz (225g) icing sugar

Preheat the oven to 350°F/180°C/Gas 4. Grease and base-line two 8in (20cm) sandwich tins.

Break the chocolate into small pieces and put into a bowl with the water over hot water. Heat gently until melted. Sieve the flour and cocoa together. Cream the butter and sugar until soft and fluffy. Add the essence and chocolate. Separate the eggs and beat the yolks into the chocolate mixture. Fold in the flour mixture and milk. Whisk the egg whites to stiff peaks and fold into the mixture. Divide between the tins and bake for 30 minutes. Turn out on to a wire rack to cool.

To make the filling, melt the chocolate in a bowl over a pan of hot water. Add the evaporated milk and beat over the heat until light and creamy. Remove from the heat and leave to cool for 5 minutes, stirring often. Sieve the icing sugar and work into the chocolate mixture. When thick and smooth, sandwich the cakes together with one-third of the icing. Spread the rest over the surface of the cake.

Chocolate Teabread

*

This chocolate-flavoured fruit loaf may be eaten plain, or is even more delicious spread with unsalted butter.

Ingredients

FOR A 2LB (900G) LOAF CAKE

9oz (250g) self-raising flour
4oz (100g) butter or hard margarine
4oz (100g) caster sugar
2oz (50g) seedless raisins
2oz (50g) currants
1oz (25g) chopped mixed peel
2 eggs
2oz (50g) plain chocolate
3–4 tbs milk

Preheat the oven to 350°F/180°C/Gas 4. Grease and base-line a 2lb (900g) loaf tin. Sieve the flour into a bowl. Rub in the fat until the mixture is like fine breadcrumbs. Stir in the sugar, raisins, currants and peel. Beat the eggs lightly and stir into the mixture. Melt the chocolate in a pan over hot water and add to the mixture. Beat well, adding enough milk to make a soft dropping consistency. Put into the prepared tin and bake for 1 hour. Cool in the tin for 3 minutes and turn on to a wire rack to cool.

Austrian Chocolate Cake

— ★ —

Austrian cooks have a way with rich chocolate cakes. This one has a particularly light texture and is very rich.

Ingredients

FOR A 8IN (20CM) CAKE

8oz (225g) plain chocolate
8oz (225g) unsalted butter
8oz (225g) dark soft brown sugar
6 eggs
8oz (225g) ground almonds
8oz (225g) fresh white breadcrumbs
2 teasp coffee powder

FILLING

4 tbs apricot jam

ICING

5oz (125g) plain chocolate
1 tbs caster sugar
3 tbs water

Preheat the oven to 375°F/190°F/Gas 5. Grease and base-line two 8in (20cm) sandwich tins. Put the chocolate into a bowl over a pan of hot water and heat gently until melted. Leave to cool. Cream the butter and sugar until light and fluffy, and gradually beat in the eggs one at a time. Whisk in the melted chocolate and gradually add the almonds. Stir in the breadcrumbs and coffee powder. Spoon into the tins and bake for 25 minutes. Leave to cool in the tins and then turn one cake on to a serving plate.

Spread lightly with the apricot jam. Cover with the second cake. To make the icing, put the chocolate, sugar and 2 tbs water into a pan and heat very gently until melted. Take off the heat and stir in the remaining water. Beat well and cool slightly before pouring over the cake.

Chocolate Whisky Cake

— ★★ —

A wonderful blending of flavours make this a very rich and completely irresistible cake, which may be eaten at the end of a meal.

Ingredients

FOR AN 8IN (20CM) CAKE

2oz (50g) seedless raisins
4 tbs whisky
7oz (200g) plain chocolate
2 tbs water
4oz (100g) unsalted butter
3 eggs
5oz (125g) light soft brown sugar
2oz (50g) plain flour
3oz (75g) ground almonds
pinch of salt

ICING

6oz (175g) plain chocolate
6fl oz (175ml) double cream

Put the raisins into a bowl with the whisky and leave to soak overnight. Preheat the oven to 350°F/180°F/Gas 4. Grease and line a loose-bottomed 8in (20cm) round tin. Break the chocolate into small pieces and put into a bowl with the water. Heat gently until melted. Cut the butter into small pieces, and add gradually to the chocolate, stirring until smooth. Remove from the heat.

Separate the eggs and beat the yolks and sugar until pale and fluffy. Slowly pour in the chocolate mixture, stirring well until evenly coloured. Stir in the flour, almonds, raisins and whisky. Whisk the egg whites and salt to stiff peaks and fold into the chocolate mixture. Place in the tin and bake for 35 minutes. Leave in the tin for 5 minutes, and remove the sides of the tin. Gently slide the cake from its base on to a wire rack to cool. When cold, carefully peel off the lining paper and put the cake on to a serving plate.

To make the icing, break the chocolate into a bowl and add the cream. Heat gently over a pan of hot water until just melted. Stir until smooth, cool slightly and pour over the cake.

Chocolate Baba

**

A glorious confection for a special teatime, or for the end of a meal. This cake looks spectacular on a buffet table, but needs to be prepared the day before.

Ingredients

For 8–10

4oz (100g) seedless raisins
2oz (50g) chopped mixed peel
2oz (50g) glacé cherries
4 tbs rum
8oz (225g) plain flour
1oz (25g) cocoa powder
2 teasp baking powder
1/2 teasp salt
5oz (125g) light soft brown sugar
2 eggs
6 tbs corn oil
6 tbs milk
1/2 teasp vanilla essence

SYRUP AND TOPPING

4oz (100g) sugar
1/4pt (150ml) water
4 tbs rum
1/2pt (300ml) whipping cream
chocolate shapes

Put the raisins and peel into a bowl. Chop the cherries and mix with the other fruit. Stir in the rum and leave to soak. Preheat the oven to 350°F/180°C/Gas 4. Grease a 2½pt (1.5l) ring tin. Sieve the flour, cocoa powder, baking powder and salt into a bowl and stir in the sugar until evenly coloured. Separate the eggs, and put the yolks into a bowl with the oil, milk and essence and mix well. Add to the dry ingredients and beat well to a creamy batter. Whisk the egg whites to stiff peaks and fold into the mixture. Lightly stir in the raisins, peel, cherries and rum. Put into the tin and bake for 55 minutes. Leave in the tin for 5 minutes and turn on to a wire rack to cool.

Put the sugar and water into a heavy-based pan and bring them slowly to the boil. Simmer for 5 minutes and then take off the heat and stir in the rum. When the cake is cold, return it to the tin and spoon over the hot syrup. Cover and leave overnight.

Just before serving, whip the cream to soft peaks. Turn out the cake on to a serving dish. Pipe the cream in lines and decorate with chocolate shapes. Serve at once.

Never-fail Chocolate Cake

*

A very easy cake prepared in two layers which may be filled with chocolate or coffee butter icing, but is just as good if layered with apricot or raspberry jam and topped with melted plain chocolate.

Ingredients
FOR A 7IN (17.5CM) ROUND CAKE

6oz (175g) soft margarine
6oz (175g) caster sugar
6oz (175g) self-raising flour
1 teasp baking powder
1oz (25g) cocoa powder
3 eggs
2 tbs milk

ICING

4oz (100g) soft margarine
6oz (175g) icing sugar
1oz (25g) cocoa powder
2 tbs boiling water

Preheat the oven to 350°F/180°C/Gas 4. Grease and base-line two 7in (17.5cm) sponge sandwich tins.

Put the margarine, sugar, flour, baking powder, cocoa powder, eggs and milk into a bowl and beat hard until very light and creamy. Divide between the two tins and bake for 30 minutes. Turn on to a wire rack to cool.

To make the icing, put the margarine and sugar into a bowl and beat until creamy. Mix the cocoa powder with boiling water and gradually beat into the creamed mixture. Leave until cold before sandwiching the cake layers together and spreading the remaining icing on the top of the cake.

Chocolate Chip Orange Cake

**

Chocolate and orange provide a sophisticated flavour combination for a delicious but simple cake with a soft icing.

Ingredients
FOR A 7IN (17.5CM) ROUND CAKE

6oz (175g) butter
8oz (225g) caster sugar
4 eggs
10oz (300g) plain flour
1 teasp baking powder
grated rind of 1 orange
2oz (50g) plain chocolate

ICING

4oz (100g) plain chocolate
3 tbs water
1 teasp salad oil
1 oz (25g) caster sugar
9 crystallised orange slices

Preheat the oven to 350°F/180°C/Gas 4. Grease and base-line a 7in (17.5cm) round cake tin.

Cream together the butter and sugar until light and fluffy. Beat the eggs lightly. Sieve together the flour and baking powder. Add the eggs and flour alternately to the creamed mixture, beating well between each addition. Chop the chocolate into small pieces, and fold the orange rind and chocolate into the cake mixture. Put into the prepared tin and bake for 1¼ hours. Turn on to a wire rack to cool.

To prepare the icing, break the chocolate into small pieces and put into a heavy-based pan with the water, oil and sugar. Heat gently, stirring until the chocolate has melted and the mixture is smooth. Cool for 5 minutes, stir well and pour over the cake. Arrange orange slices on top.

Panforte

**

A rich, chewy confection from Siena, which has many varieties. This chocolate-flavoured version is rich with honey, nuts and glacé fruit.

Ingredients
FOR A 10IN (25CM) CAKE

6oz (175g) hazelnuts
6oz (175g) blanched split almonds
3oz (75g) glacé pineapple
3oz (75g) glacé apricots
2oz (50g) glacé cherries
2oz (50g) chopped mixed candied peel
3oz (75g) plain flour
1½oz (40g) cocoa powder
3 teasp ground cinnamon
12oz (350g) honey
5oz (125g) sugar

Preheat the oven to 325°F/160°C/Gas 3. Grease a 10in (25cm) round cake tin and line the base with baking parchment.

Put the hazelnuts on to a baking sheet and toast in the oven until the skins blister. Rub off the skins with a clean cloth. Put the almonds on to a baking sheet and toast in the oven until golden. Chop the hazelnuts and almonds coarsely. Chop the pineapple, apricots, cherries and peel and mix with the nuts. Stir in the flour, cocoa powder and cinnamon until evenly coloured. Put the honey and sugar into a heavy-based pan and bring to the boil. Boil until the mixture reaches 237°F/114°C (or until a little of the mixture dropped into a cup of cold water forms a soft ball). Pour over the mixture and stir well. Pour into the prepared tin and press down evenly. Bake for 30 minutes and then cool in the tin for 10 minutes. Turn on to a wire rack and peel off the baking parchment. Cool completely. Wrap in foil and store for 7 days before serving.

Chocolate Hazelnut Cake

**

This moist-textured, rich chocolate nut cake, topped by a chocolate cream icing, may be served as a cake or pudding with cream.

Ingredients
FOR A 7IN (17.5CM) CAKE

4oz (100g) unsalted butter
4oz (100g) caster sugar
3 eggs
4oz (100g) plain chocolate
5oz (125g) ground hazelnuts
1oz (25g) plain flour

ICING

¼pt (150ml) double cream
5oz (125g) plain chocolate
8 Liqueur Truffles (p98)

Preheat the oven to 350°F/180°F/Gas 4. Grease and base-line a 7in (17.5cm) spring-form tin. Butter the base paper and dust lightly with flour. Cream the butter and sugar until very light and fluffy. Separate the eggs and beat in the yolks one at a time. Melt the chocolate in a bowl over hot water and stir into the creamed mixture. Mix the nuts and flour until evenly coloured and fold into the chocolate. Whisk the egg whites to stiff peaks and fold into the mixture. Place in the prepared tin and bake for 1 hour. Leave in the tin for 5 minutes and turn on to a wire rack to cool.

To make the icing, put the cream into a heavy-based pan and heat to just under boiling point. Add the chocolate and stir until thick and smooth. Take off the heat, and stir well until very creamy. Put the cake on to a serving plate and pour over the icing. When set (after about 1 hour), decorate with Liqueur Truffles.

Triple Cake
★★

Three ways of using plain chocolate in a rich cake, with a sponge layered with smooth chocolate buttercream and topped with mocha cream icing.

Ingredients
FOR A 6IN (15CM) CAKE

3 eggs
3oz (75g) caster sugar
2oz (50g) plain chocolate
3oz (75g) plain flour

FILLING

2oz (50g) caster sugar
4 tbs water
2 egg yolks
5oz (125g) unsalted butter
1½oz (40g) plain chocolate

ICING

4 tbs double cream
1 tbs strong black coffee
2½oz (65g) plain chocolate

Preheat the oven to 350°F/180°C/Gas 4. Grease and line a 6in (15cm) round cake tin. Grease the lining paper and dust lightly with flour. Separate the eggs and whisk the yolks and sugar until very pale and thick. Melt the chocolate in a bowl over a pan of hot water. Fold into the egg mixture. Whisk the egg whites to stiff peaks and fold into the mixture alternately with the flour. Put into the prepared tin and bake for 35 minutes. Cool in the tin for 5 minutes and turn on to a wire rack to cool.

Prepare the buttercream by putting the sugar and water into a heavy-based pan. Dissolve the sugar over low heat and cook over medium heat to 215°F/102°C or until a little of the mixture forms a thin thread from the spoon (see Cook's Tip, p.22). Whisk the egg yolks until thick and creamy and gradually whisk in the hot syrup until the mixture is fluffy and cool. Beat the butter in another bowl until light and creamy and gradually beat in the egg mixture until thick and shiny. Melt the chocolate in a bowl over hot water, cool and stir into the buttercream.

Split the cake into three layers and reassemble with the buttercream between each layer. Put the cream and coffee into a heavy-based pan and bring just to the boil. Break the chocolate into small pieces and stir into the cream until melted. Remove from the heat and continue stirring until cool and smooth. Pour over the cake and leave to stand for 15 minutes.

Truffle Roll
★★

A chocolate Swiss roll with a rum truffle filling is rolled in grated chocolate and garnished with truffle sweets.

Ingredients
FOR 1 CAKE

4 eggs
4oz (100g) caster sugar
2oz (50g) plain flour
1½oz (40g) cocoa powder

FILLING AND TOPPING

6 fl oz (175ml) double cream
1 tbs rum
5oz (125g) plain chocolate
3oz (75g) grated plain chocolate
8 chocolate truffles

Preheat the oven to 450°F/230°C/Gas 8. Grease and base-line a 12x9in (30x22.5cm) Swiss-roll tin, and lightly grease and flour the paper.

Separate the eggs and whisk the egg yolks and sugar until very pale and thick. Sieve the flour and cocoa powder together. Whisk the egg whites to stiff peaks and fold into the egg mixture alternately with the flour. Fill the tin and bake for 12 minutes. Put a clean tea towel on to a flat surface and cover with a piece of greaseproof paper lightly dusted with caster sugar. Turn the cooked cake on to this and peel off the lining paper. Trim the crisp edges from the cake. Put a piece of greaseproof paper on top of the cake and roll up carefully. Cover with a damp tea towel and leave until cold.

Prepare the filling by putting the cream and rum into a heavy-based pan and bringing just to the boil. Break the chocolate into small pieces and stir into the pan. When the chocolate has melted, remove from heat and stir well until thick and smooth. Chill for 1 hour and then whisk until light and fluffy.

Unroll the cake and spread lightly with half the filling mixture. Roll up gently. Spread the remaining mixture lightly over the surface of the cake, including the ends. Coat completely with grated chocolate. Put on to a serving dish and arrange a line of chocolate truffles down the centre. Serve each slice of cake with a chocolate truffle.

Chocolate Ginger Cup Cakes

*

Small light sponge cakes are delicious freshly baked, and make a good emergency pudding served warm with ice cream.

Ingredients

FOR 18 CAKES

4oz (100g) butter
4oz (100g) caster sugar
2 eggs
4oz (100g) self-raising flour
1 teasp ground ginger
2oz (50g) chocolate chips

Preheat the oven to 350°F/180°C/Gas 4. Place paper baking cases in tartlet tins so that they keep their shape.

Cream the butter and sugar until light and fluffy. Beat the eggs. Sieve the flour with the ginger. Add eggs and flour alternately to the creamed mixture, and beat well. Spoon the mixture into baking cases. Sprinkle chocolate chips on each one. Bake for 20 minutes. Cool on a wire rack.

Assorted Truffles (pp98-101)
Chocolate Baba (p76)
Chocolate Marble Cake (p71)
Chocolate Liègeois (p119)

Cup Cakes

**

Nursery favourites with a deep chocolate flavour and soft, smooth icing.

Ingredients

FOR 30 CAKES

1oz (25g) cocoa powder
2 tbs boiling water
4oz (100g) soft margarine
6oz (175g) caster sugar
6oz (175g) self-raising flour
1 teasp baking powder
2 eggs
4 tbs milk

ICING

4oz (100g) plain chocolate
4 tbs water
1oz (25g) unsalted butter
6oz (175g) icing sugar

Preheat the oven to 350°F/180°C/Gas 4. Put 30 paper cake cases into patty tins.

Put the cocoa into a large bowl and add the boiling water. Mix well and leave to stand for 5 minutes. Add the margarine, sugar, flour, baking powder, eggs and milk. Beat hard until well mixed and creamy. Divide between the paper cases and bake for 15 minutes. Leave to cool in the tins.

To make the icing, break the chocolate into small pieces and put into a bowl over hot water. Add the water and butter and melt gently. Take off the heat and beat in the icing sugar. Cool slightly and pour on top of each cake. Leave until cold and set before removing cakes from tins.

Chocolate Fruit Celebration Cake

*

Those who are addicted to chocolate on all occasions might like to serve this as a Christmas cake or even a wedding cake.

Ingredients

FOR AN 8 IN (20CM) SQUARE CAKE

350g (12oz) sultanas
6oz (175g) glacé cherries
6oz (175g) glacé apricots
6oz (175g) plain chocolate
7oz (200g) unsalted butter
5oz (125g) light soft brown sugar
8fl oz (225ml) sweet sherry
4 eggs
6oz (175g) chocolate chips
7oz (200g) plain flour
1oz (25g) self-raising flour
½ teasp bicarbonate of soda

Preheat the oven to 300°F/150°C/Gas 2. Grease and line the base and sides of an 8in (20cm) square cake tin.

Put the sultanas, halved cherries and chopped apricots into a heavy-based pan. Add the chocolate broken into small pieces with the butter and sugar. Reserve 2 tbs sherry and put the rest into the pan. Heat gently until the chocolate and butter have melted. Bring to the boil, and then simmer for 10 minutes. Turn into a large bowl and leave until lukewarm.

Beat the eggs into the fruit mixture and then beat in the chocolate chips, flours and soda. Spread in the tin and bake for 2½ hours. Brush with reserved sherry, cover with foil and cool in the tin. Turn out when cold.

Sicilian Chocolate Squares

**

This incredibly light chocolate cake sandwiched with a luscious cream cheese filling can only be eaten in very small portions.

Ingredients
FOR 16 SQUARES

3 eggs
3 tbs caster sugar
2 tbs cocoa powder
few drops of vanilla essence

FILLING

3oz (75g) cream cheese
3 tbs icing sugar
2 tbs orange liqueur
2 tbs chopped mixed candied peel
1½oz (40g) plain chocolate
cocoa powder

Preheat the oven to 350°F/180°C/Gas 4. Grease a 12x8in (30x20cm) Swiss-roll tin and line the base with greaseproof paper. Grease the paper and sprinkle lightly with flour. Shake off excess flour.

Separate the eggs and beat the yolks with sugar until light and fluffy. Fold in the cocoa powder and vanilla essence. Whisk the egg whites to stiff peaks and fold into the mixture. Spread lightly to cover the base of the tin. Bake for 12 minutes. Cool in the tin for 10 minutes. Turn out on to a piece of greaseproof paper, and peel the paper from the base.

Beat the cream cheese until very light. Stir in the sugar and liqueur. Chop the peel very finely, and grate the chocolate finely. Add to the cheese mixture. Trim the hard edges from the sheet of cake, and cut the cake in half. Spread the filling over one piece of cake and top with the other half, pressing lightly together. Sift cocoa powder lightly over the top. Chill in the refrigerator for 2 hours and cut into squares. Store covered in the refrigerator for up to 48 hours.

Truffle Cakes

*

Richly-flavoured gooey balls of chocolate cake which are very addictive, but incredibly easy to make.

Ingredients
FOR 12–15 CAKES

1lb (450g) stale cake
syrup from canned fruit (or weak orange squash)
1oz (25g) cocoa powder (optional)
2–3oz (50–75g) seedless raisins (optional)
2–3 tbs rum
4oz (100g) apricot jam
3 tbs water
8oz (225g) chocolate vermicelli

Any type of cake may be used, or a mixture of cakes such as chocolate, sponge cake and fruit cake. If there is plenty of chocolate cake, no cocoa powder will be needed; if there is plenty of fruit cake, the raisins may be omitted. Break the cake into crumbs and put into a large bowl with the cocoa and raisins, if used. Sprinkle with some syrup from canned fruit, or some weak orange squash to moisten the crumbs, but not to make them soggy. Leave in a cool place for 30 minutes. Stir in the rum. Mix well and form the damp crumbs into round, firm balls.

Put the apricot jam and water into a heavy-based pan and bring to the boil, stirring well. Leave to stand for 5 minutes.

Meanwhile, spread the chocolate vermicelli on a plate. Using two spoons, dip each cake ball into the apricot jam until completely coated. Drain well and toss in vermicelli until completely coated. Put cakes in a single layer on a tray and leave for 2 hours until firm. Put into paper cake cases to serve.

Chocolate Meringues
*

These meringues should not be filled with cream as they are already rich enough. They make good sweetmeats for wedding receptions and similar parties.

Ingredients
For 24–30 meringues

2 egg whites
pinch of cream of tartar
pinch of salt
6oz ((175g) caster sugar
6oz (175g) plain chocolate chips

Preheat the oven to 300°F/150°C/Gas 2. Base-line two baking sheets with baking parchment. Whisk the egg whites, cream of tartar and salt to stiff peaks. Gradually add the sugar, whisking all the time, until the mixture stands in stiff peaks and is thick and shiny. Fold in the chocolate chips. Drop the mixture in large rounded teaspoonfuls on to the baking sheets, and bake for 30 minutes.

Carefully lift off the meringues and return them to the baking sheets with the flat bases upwards. Bake for 15 minutes. Turn off the oven and leave in the meringues for 30 minutes. Remove from the tins and leave on a wire rack until cold. Store in an airtight tin.

Crunch Brownies
*

Plain chocolate cake with a rich, soft texture contrasts with a sugared nut topping.

Ingredients
For 16 squares

8oz (225g) self-raising flour
1 teasp ground cinnamon
pinch of salt
4oz (100g) soft margarine
4oz (100g) dark soft brown sugar
3oz (75g) plain chocolate
5oz (125g) golden syrup
1 teasp bicarbonate of soda
2 tbs milk

TOPPING

4oz (100g) plain flour
2oz (50g) butter
1oz (25g) demerara sugar
2oz (50g) chopped walnuts

Preheat the oven to 375°F/190°C/Gas 5. Grease and base-line a deep 11x7in (27.5x17.5cm) tin.

Sieve the flour, cinnamon and salt together. Cream the fat and sugar until light and fluffy. Melt the chocolate and golden syrup together. Stir in the bicarbonate of soda and milk, and add alternately to the creamed mixture with the flour. Beat well and put into the tin.

Make the topping by rubbing the butter into the flour, and stirring in the sugar and walnuts. Sprinkle over the cake. Bake for 45 minutes. Cool in the tin and cut into squares.

Syrup Brownies

**

Another version of this popular American cookie which has a particularly fudge-like consistency.

Ingredients
FOR 12 SQUARES

4oz (100g) sugar
¼pt (150ml) water
1oz (25g) cocoa powder
4oz (100g) unsalted butter
8oz (225g) light soft brown sugar
2 egg yolks
6oz (175g) plain flour
¼ teasp bicarbonate of soda
pinch of salt
3oz (75g) walnuts

Put the sugar and water into a heavy-based pan and stir over low heat until the sugar has dissolved. Bring to the boil and boil gently to 215°F/102°C (or until a little of the mixture dropped into a cup of cold water forms fine threads). Take off the heat and stir in the cocoa. Stir over low heat for 2 minutes and leave to cool.

Preheat the oven to 350°F/180°C/Gas 4. Grease an 11x7in (27.5x17.5cm) tin. Cream the butter and sugar together until light and fluffy. Beat in the egg yolks one at a time, and stir in the chocolate syrup. Sieve the flour, soda and salt together and fold into the chocolate mixture. Chop the walnuts finely and stir into the mixture. Put into the tin and bake for 40 minutes. Leave in the tin for 5 minutes and turn on to a wire rack to cool. Cut into squares.

Chocolate Fudge Squares

*

Careful timing is needed for baking these biscuits to achieve the perfect texture.

Ingredients
FOR 24 BISCUITS

4oz (100g) soft margarine
2oz (50g) dark soft brown sugar
4oz (100g) self-raising flour
2oz (50g) porridge oats
3 teasp cocoa powder

ICING

4oz (100g) icing sugar
3 teasp cocoa powder
5 teasp lukewarm water

Preheat the oven to 325°F/160°C/Gas 3. Grease an 11x7in (27.5x17.5cm) shallow tin. Put the margarine and sugar into a bowl and cream them until soft and well mixed. Work in the flour, oats and cocoa and mix well until evenly coloured. Press into the tin, using a fork to spread the mixture evenly. Bake for exactly 30 minutes (no longer, or the biscuits become hard and unpalatable).

Mix the icing ingredients until smooth and evenly coloured. As soon as the tin is removed from the oven, leave to cool for exactly 5 minutes, then pour over the icing. Leave in the tin until completely cold and set. Cut into squares or fingers and store in an airtight tin.

Chocolate Macaroons
*

Delicious chocolate almond morsels for teatime, or to serve with creamy puddings.

Ingredients
For 12 MACAROONS

2 egg whites
8oz (225g) caster sugar
4½oz (115g) ground almonds
1½oz (40g) drinking chocolate powder
edible rice paper
blanched almonds

Preheat the oven to 350°F/180°C/Gas 4. Cover two baking sheets with rice paper. Whisk the egg whites to stiff peaks. Stir the sugar, almonds and chocolate powder together until evenly coloured. Fold into the egg whites. Place in small spoonfuls on the rice paper, leaving room for spreading.

Place an almond on each biscuit. Bake for 20 minutes. Lift carefully on to a wire rack to cool. When cold, trim off surplus rice paper round the edge of each macaroon. Store in an airtight tin.

Chocolate Flapjacks
*

Simple family favourites become irresistible when chocolate is added.

Ingredients
For 12 FLAPJACKS

4oz (100g) butter
1oz (25g) light soft brown sugar
2 tbs golden syrup
8oz (225g) porridge oats
3oz (75g) plain chocolate

Preheat the oven to 350°F/180°C/Gas 4. Put the butter, sugar and syrup into a pan and heat gently until the fat has melted. Remove from the heat and stir in the oats. Chop the chocolate finely and stir into the mixture. Press into a greased 11x7in (27.5x17.5cm) tin. Bake for 25 minutes. Cool and mark into squares. When nearly cold, cut firmly and lift on to a wire rack to cool.

One-pot Brownies
*

One of the easiest recipes for these popular cookies, but one of the best. They are very addictive, but especially good for tucking into a lunchbox or picnic hamper.

Ingredients
For 24 BROWNIES

3oz (75g) butter or hard margarine
8oz (225g) granulated sugar
2 eggs
½ teasp vanilla essence
3 heaped tbs cocoa powder
2oz (50g) plain flour
1 teasp baking powder
4oz (100g) chopped walnuts
4oz (100g) seedless raisins

Preheat the oven to 350°F/180°C/Gas 4. Line an 11x7in (27.5x17.5cm) tin with foil and grease it lightly.

Melt the fat in a large pan. Cool to lukewarm and beat in all the other ingredients. Spread in the tin and bake for 30 minutes. Leave in the tin for 15 minutes. Mark into squares or fingers and remove from the tin. Leave to cool on a wire rack.

Picnic Bars

*

Crunchy bars with a chocolate and cherry topping are perfect for packed meals but just as good with a glass of milk or cup of coffee.

Ingredients

FOR 16 BARS

2oz (50g) butter
2oz (50g) white vegetable fat
10oz (300g) light soft brown sugar
5¹/₂oz (150g) plain flour
2 eggs
1 teasp baking powder
pinch of salt
4oz (100g) chocolate chips
4oz (100g) glacé cherries

Preheat the oven to 350°F/180°C/Gas 4. Grease an 11x7in (27.5x17.5cm) tin. Cream together the butter, white fat and 3oz (75g) sugar. Stir in 4oz (100g) flour and mix well. Press into the prepared tin and bake for 10 minutes. Beat together lightly the eggs and remaining sugar and stir in the remaining flour, baking powder and salt. Stir in the chocolate chips. Chop the cherries roughly and add to the mixture.

Spread over the partly cooked base and continue baking for 30 minutes. Cool in the tin. Cut into 16 bars and put on to a wire rack to finish cooling.

Chocolate Marshmallow Shortbread

**

An addictive mixture of rich shortbread, a soft filling studded with nuts and glacé fruit, and a plain chocolate topping.

Ingredients

FOR 30 PIECES

4oz (100g) plain flour
pinch of salt
3oz (75g) unsalted butter
2 tbs icing sugar
1 egg yolk

FILLING

1 tbs double cream
7oz (200g) marshmallows
3oz (75g) walnuts
2oz (50g) glacé cherries
1oz (25g) angelica

TOPPING

4oz (100g) plain chocolate
1oz (25g) unsalted butter

Preheat the oven to 350°F/180°C/Gas 4. Grease an 11x7in (27.5x17.5cm) tin. Sieve flour and salt into a bowl and rub in butter lightly until the mixture is like coarse breadcrumbs. Stir in the icing sugar and egg yolk. Mix well and press into the tin in an even layer. Prick well with a fork and chill for 20 minutes. Bake for 20 minutes and leave to cool in the tin.

Put the cream in a small pan with the marshmallows and heat gently until melted. Chop the walnuts, cherries and angelica. Stir into the pan, remove from heat and spread over the shortbread. Leave until cold and set.

Put the chocolate and butter into a bowl

over a pan of hot water and heat gently until the chocolate has melted. Stir well and spread quickly over the marshmallow layer. Leave until set. Cut into small pieces. For storage, wrap the tin and store in the refrigerator for up to 7 days.

No-bake Chocolate Squares
*

A good way of using leftover biscuits to make a rich teatime treat.

Ingredients
FOR 16 SQUARES

6oz (175g) mixed sweet biscuits
2oz (50g) hazelnuts
2oz (50g) seedless raisins
3oz (75g) unsalted butter
2 tbs golden syrup
6 oz (150g) plain chocolate

Grease an 8in (20cm) square tin.

Crush the biscuits, but not too finely. Chop the nuts and mix with the biscuit crumbs and raisins. Put the butter and syrup into a small pan and add 2oz (50g) chocolate. Heat gently until melted and stir into the crumb mixture. Mix well and press into the tin in an even layer. Leave until cold and hard. Put the remaining chocolate into a bowl over hot water and heat gently until melted. Pour over the biscuit mixture and leave to harden. Cut into squares and remove from the tin.

Turtles
**

Shortbread with a thick caramel topping, completed by a coating of plain chocolate and crunchy nuts.

Ingredients
FOR 15 SQUARES

4oz (100g) soft margarine
2oz (50g) caster sugar
6oz (175g) plain flour

TOPPING

4oz (100g) hard margarine
3oz (75g) caster sugar
2 tbs golden syrup
7oz (200g) can sweetened condensed milk

COATING

4oz (100g) plain chocolate
2oz (50g) hazelnuts or walnuts

Preheat the oven to 350°F/180°C/Gas 4. Grease an 11x7in (27.5x17.5cm) tin.

Work the soft margarine, sugar and flour together to make a firm dough. Press into the tin to give an even layer and prick with a fork. Bake for 25 minutes.

While the base is cooking, prepare the topping. Put the margarine, sugar, syrup and condensed milk into a heavy-based pan and heat gently until melted. Boil for 7–8 minutes until the mixture is caramel coloured, stirring well so that the mixture does not burn. Remove from heat and cool to lukewarm.

Remove the shortbread from the oven and leave to cool in the tin for 5 minutes. Pour over the topping and leave until cold.

Melt the chocolate in a bowl over a pan of hot water. Pour over the caramel and mark in lines with a fork. Sprinkle with finely chopped nuts. Leave until cold before cutting.

Hungarian Mocha Cookies

**

A subtle blend of chocolate and coffee makes these lovely filled biscuits suitable for a special tea party. The filling is nicest when it is not too sweet.

Ingredients

FOR 20 COOKIES

8oz (225g) unsalted butter
4oz (100g) caster sugar
8oz (225g) self-raising flour
2oz (50g) cocoa powder

FILLING

2oz (50g) cocoa powder
¼pt (150ml) strong black coffee
2oz (50g) unsalted butter
caster sugar to taste

Preheat the oven to 350°F/180°C/Gas 4. Grease two baking sheets.

Cream the butter and sugar until light and fluffy. Stir the flour and cocoa together until evenly coloured, and then work into the creamed mixture. With the hands, form the mixture into balls the size of a large walnut. Place the pieces on the baking sheets, leaving a little space between them. Dip a fork into cold water and press the biscuits down lightly. Bake for 12 minutes and lift carefully on to a wire rack to cool.

To make the filling, put the cocoa into a small pan with the coffee. Heat gently, stirring well, until the mixture is a thick cream. Take off the heat and beat in the butter. Add sugar to taste, but do not oversweeten. When the mixture is cold, sandwich the biscuits together in pairs. If liked, the tops may be dusted with sieved icing sugar just before serving.

Chocolate Chip Walnut Cookies

*

An unbeatable combination of plain chocolate and walnut pieces in a crisp biscuit casing. These are especially good with a glass of milk or cup of coffee.

Ingredients

FOR 40–50 BISCUITS

3oz (75g) butter
3oz (75g) dark soft brown sugar
3oz (75g) granulated sugar
½ teasp vanilla essence
6oz (175g) self-raising flour
pinch of salt
1 egg
4oz (100g) plain chocolate chips
2oz (50g) chopped walnuts

Preheat the oven to 350°F/180°C/Gas 4. Grease two baking sheets.

Cream the butter and sugars until light and fluffy, and work in the essence. Mix the flour and salt and work into the creamed mixture with the beaten egg. Stir in the chocolate chips and walnuts until evenly mixed. Drop teaspoonfuls of the mixture on to the baking sheets, leaving room for the biscuits to spread. Bake for 10 minutes. Lift carefully on to a wire rack to cool. Store in an airtight tin.

Viennese Chocolate Shells

**

Biscuits with a very short texture and a simple filling which enhances the chocolate flavour.

Ingredients
For 12 biscuits

5oz (125g) unsalted butter
3oz (75g) caster sugar
7oz (200g) self-raising flour
1oz (25g) cornflour
3oz (75g) plain chocolate
2oz (50g) apricot jam
icing sugar

Preheat the oven to 375°F/190°C/Gas 5. Grease two baking sheets.

Cream the butter and sugar until light and fluffy. Sieve the flour and cornflour together and work into the creamed mixture. Melt the chocolate in a bowl over hot water. Cool slightly and work into the mixture.

Put into a piping bag fitted with a large star nozzle, and pipe out shell shapes on the baking sheets. Bake for 15 minutes. Cool on a wire rack.

Sandwich the biscuits together in pairs with the jam and sprinkle the top surfaces with sieved icing sugar.

Hazelnut Crisps

*

These chocolate nut biscuits are very good with ice cream.

Ingredients
For 40 biscuits

4oz (100g) butter or margarine
4oz (100g) caster sugar
6oz (175g) plain flour
2oz (50g) ground hazelnuts
2oz (50g) plain chocolate
1 egg white
1½ oz (40g) shelled hazelnuts

Preheat the oven to 375°F/190°C/Gas 5. Grease two baking sheets.

Cream the fat and sugar together until light and fluffy. Work in the flour and ground hazelnuts. Chop the chocolate finely and work into the mixture, with a little egg white if necessary to bind to a firm paste.

Roll out and cut into rounds or other shapes. Whisk the egg white and brush over the biscuits. Arrange shelled nuts on each one. Bake for 20 minutes, and lift on to a wire rack to cool.

Chocolate Lemon Bourbons

*

The traditional Bourbon biscuit is given extra flavour with ground almonds and a hint of lemon rind.

Ingredients
FOR 12 BISCUITS

3oz (75g) butter
3oz (75g) caster sugar
3oz (75g) plain flour
3oz (75g) ground almonds
grated rind of 1 lemon
2oz (50g) plain chocolate

FILLING

2oz (50g) butter
4oz (100g) icing sugar
1/2oz (15g) cocoa powder

icing sugar

Preheat the oven to 375°F/190°C/Gas 5. Grease two baking sheets.

Cream the butter and sugar until light and fluffy. Work in the flour, ground almonds and lemon rind. Melt the chocolate in a bowl over hot water. Cool slightly and work into the mixture. Roll out and cut into rectangles. Place on the baking sheets and prick each biscuit three or four times with a fork. Bake for 20 minutes. Cool on a wire rack.

To make the filling, cream the butter, icing sugar and cocoa powder together until smooth and light. Sandwich the biscuits together in pairs and sprinkle the top surfaces with sieved icing sugar.

Chocolate Rings

*

Rich chocolate biscuits dipped in plain chocolate are the perfect accompaniment to milk or coffee, or they may be used as a base for serving ice creams or sorbets.

Ingredients
FOR 36 BISCUITS

4oz (100g) unsalted butter
4oz (100g) caster sugar
1 egg
few drops of vanilla essence
8oz (225g) plain flour
1oz (25g) cocoa powder
6oz (175g) plain chocolate

Preheat the oven to 375°F/190°C/Gas 5. Grease two baking sheets.

Cream the butter and sugar until light and fluffy. Beat in the egg and essence. Work in the flour and cocoa. Chill for 30 minutes, and roll out. Cut into 2½in (6.25cm) rounds. Remove centres with a small round cutter and re-roll until all dough is used. Bake for 15 minutes, and cool on a wire rack.

Put the chocolate into a bowl over hot water, and heat gently until melted. Dip each biscuit into the chocolate until coated, and place on a sheet of baking parchment until cold and set.

Florentines

**

Crisp fruit and nut biscuits contrast with smooth dark chocolate. They are perfect for a wedding reception or special party.

Ingredients
FOR 20 BISCUITS

3oz (75g) blanched almonds
1¹/₂oz (40g) glacé cherries
2oz (50g) unsalted butter
3oz (75g) caster sugar
1oz (25g) flaked almonds
2oz (50g) chopped mixed peel
2 tbs double cream
4oz (100g) plain chocolate

Preheat the oven to 350°F/180°C/Gas 4. Line 2 baking sheets with baking parchment. Chop the blanched almonds and quarter the cherries. Put the butter into a pan and stir in the sugar. Bring slowly to the boil. Remove the butter from the heat and stir in the chopped and flaked almonds, peel, cherries and cream.

Put teaspoonfuls far apart on the baking sheets. Bake for 8–10 minutes until golden-brown. Neaten the edges with a knife to form circles. Cool slightly and lift on to a wire rack to cool.

Melt the chocolate in a bowl over a pan of hot water. Spread on the smooth side of the biscuits and mark with a fork in wavy lines. Leave for 15 minutes to set.

Chocolate Chip Raisin Cookies

*

Tempting cookies which are particularly good eaten freshly baked and still slightly warm.

Ingredients
FOR 15 COOKIES

4oz (100g) butter
4oz (100g) light soft brown sugar
2oz (50g) caster sugar
1 egg
few drops of vanilla essence
6oz (175g) plain flour
¹/₂ teasp salt
¹/₂ teasp bicarbonate of soda
4oz (100g) plain chocolate chips
4oz (100g) seedless raisins

Preheat the oven to 325°F/160°C/Gas 3. Grease two baking sheets.

Cream together the butter, brown sugar and caster sugar until light and fluffy. Beat in the egg and vanilla essence. Sieve the flour with salt and soda and work into the creamed mixture. Fold in the chocolate chips and raisins. Form into 15 balls and place at intervals on the baking sheets, allowing room for spreading. Press down lightly with a fork dipped in cold water. Bake for 18 minutes. Cool for 2 minutes and lift on to a wire rack to finish cooling.

Chocolate Chip Shortbread

★

Traditional shortbread with contrasting pieces of chocolate and flaked almonds.

Ingredients
FOR A 6IN (15CM) SHORTBREAD ROUND

4oz (100g) unsalted butter
2oz (50g) caster sugar
6oz (175g) plain flour
2oz (50g) rice flour or cornflour
4oz (100g) chocolate chips
1oz (25g) flaked almonds
icing sugar

Preheat the oven to 300°F/150°C/Gas 2. Butter and flour a flan ring and place on a greased baking sheet.

Rub together the butter, sugar, flour and rice flour or cornflour to make a smooth, firm paste. Work in the chocolate chips. Press into the flan ring and press down lightly with a fork. Sprinkle with flaked almonds. Bake for 40 minutes until very pale gold in colour. Leave to stand until cold. Lift on to a serving plate and dust lightly with icing sugar. For convenience of serving, the shortbread may be marked lightly into triangles before it cools.

Chocolate Coconut Bars

★

Useful cookies to have in the tin for emergencies, with the slightly crunchy base contrasting with smooth chocolate.

Ingredients
FOR 12–16 BARS

4oz (100g) unsalted butter
6oz (150g) caster sugar
2 eggs
4oz (100g) ground rice
4oz (100g) desiccated coconut
4oz (100g) sultanas
4oz (100g) glacé cherries
6oz (175g) plain chocolate

Preheat the oven to 325°F/160°C/Gas 3. Grease and base-line an 11x7in (27.5x 17.5cm) tin.

Cream the butter and sugar together until light and soft. Beat in the eggs and then stir in the ground rice, coconut, sultanas and chopped cherries. Put into the prepared tin and bake for 30 minutes. Leave to cool in the tin.

Break the chocolate into small pieces and put into a bowl over a pan of hot water. When the chocolate has melted, pour over the base. Leave until cold and firm before cutting into bars and removing from the tin.

White Chocolate Fruit Bars

*

An incredible confection of dried fruit and mixed nuts held together by white chocolate and honey, which is good with after-dinner coffee.

Ingredients
FOR 24 SQUARES

4oz (100g) flaked almonds
8oz (225g) chopped walnuts
8oz (225g) desiccated coconut
4oz (100g) currants
4oz (100g) chopped dried apricots
1oz (25g) plain flour
8oz (225g) white chocolate
6oz (175g) clear honey
6oz (175g) apricot jam
2 tbs icing sugar

Preheat the oven to 325°F/160°C/Gas 3. Grease and base-line an 8x12in (20x30cm) tin and grease the lining paper.

Put the almonds, walnuts, coconut, currants, apricots and flour into a large bowl and stir well together. Break the chocolate into small pieces and put into another bowl over hot water. Heat until melted, and then mix with the honey and jam. Stir into the dry ingredients and spread evenly in the prepared tin. Bake for 50 minutes. Cool in the tin and then sprinkle with icing sugar. Cut into small squares and remove from the tin. Store in the refrigerator.

Chocolate Maple Bars

**

A simple chocolate cake stuffed with raisins and topped with an unusual chocolate and maple syrup icing.

Ingredients
FOR 16 BARS

5oz (125g) unsalted butter
4¹/₂oz (115g) light soft brown sugar
2 eggs
2oz (50g) plain flour
1oz (25g) self-raising flour
1oz (25g) cocoa powder
¼ teasp bicarbonate of soda
4oz (100g) seedless raisins
½ teasp vanilla essence

ICING

4oz (100g) plain or milk chocolate
3 tbs maple syrup

Preheat the oven to 350°F/180°C/Gas 4. Grease and base-line an 8x12in (20x30cm) tin and grease the lining paper.

Cream the butter and sugar until light and fluffy. Beat the eggs lightly. Sieve together the flours and cocoa. Add the eggs and flour mixture alternately to the creamed mixture, beating well. Beat in the soda and raisins with the vanilla essence. Spread in the prepared tin and bake for 25 minutes. Leave to stand for 5 minutes.

For the icing, break the chocolate into small pieces in a heavy-based pan with the maple syrup. Heat gently until the chocolate has melted. Stir well and pour over the warm cake. Leave until cold before cutting into bars.

Rum Raisin Toffee Bars

**

A chocolate shortbread base is topped with rum-flavoured toffee spiked with raisins and coconut and finished with soft chocolate icing.

Ingredients
FOR 16 BARS

5oz (125g) unsalted butter
4oz (100g) caster sugar
4oz (100g) plain flour
1oz (25g) cocoa powder

TOFFEE LAYER

14oz (400g) can sweetened condensed milk
1oz (25g) unsalted butter
1 tbs rum
4oz (100g) seedless raisins
3oz (75g) desiccated coconut

TOPPING

5oz (125g) plain chocolate
1oz (25g) unsalted butter

Preheat the oven to 350°F/180°C/Gas 4. Grease and base-line an 8x12in (20x30cm) tin and grease the lining paper.

Cream the butter and sugar until light and fluffy. Sieve the flour and cocoa powder together and fold into the mixture. Press evenly into the prepared tin and bake for 20 minutes. Cool in tin for 10 minutes.

To make the toffee layer, put the condensed milk and butter into a heavy-based pan and bring to the boil, stirring all the time and then continue cooking for 10 minutes until the mixture is golden brown. Take off the heat and stir in the rum, raisins and coconut. Cool to lukewarm and spread on the cooked base.

To make the icing, put the chocolate and butter into a bowl over a pan of hot water

and heat gently until melted. Remove from the heat, stir well and spread on the cool filling. Leave until cold and set before cutting into bars.

Peanut Brownies

*

Children's favourites, which are nourishing (and non-sticky) for the lunchbox or a mid-morning snack.

Ingredients
FOR 16 SQUARES

5oz (125g) unsalted butter
4½oz (115g) dark soft brown sugar
2oz (50g) plain chocolate
2 tbs peanut butter
2 eggs
4oz (100g) unsalted roasted peanuts
3oz (75g) self-raising flour
1 tbs icing sugar

Preheat the oven to 350°F/180°C/Gas 4. Grease and base-line an 8in (20cm) square tin, and grease the lining paper.

Put the butter, sugar and chocolate into a heavy-based pan and heat gently until the chocolate has melted. Cool to lukewarm. Beat the peanut butter and eggs in a bowl and add the chopped peanuts. Stir in the chocolate mixture and the flour. Pour into the prepared tin and bake for 30 minutes.

Leave in the tin for 5 minutes and turn on to a wire rack to cool. When cold, sprinkle with icing sugar and cut into squares.

Chocolate Croissants

**

A special treat for French children is equally appreciated by adults for a leisurely breakfast with good cup of coffee.

Ingredients

FOR 8–10 CROISSANTS

6fl oz (175ml) milk
½oz (15g) fresh yeast or ¼oz (7g) dried yeast
1 teasp caster sugar
10oz (300g) bread flour
5oz (125g) butter
4oz (100g) plain chocolate
beaten egg for glazing

Warm the milk to lukewarm and mix with the yeast and sugar. Leave to stand until bubbling strongly. Sieve the flour into a warm mixing bowl and add the milk and 1oz (25g) melted butter. Mix to a soft dough and knead lightly until smooth. Place in a lightly oiled bowl, cover with a cloth and leave in a warm place for about 30 minutes until doubled in size. Knead again and roll lightly into a rectangle three times as long as wide.

Soften, but do not melt, the remaining butter, and divide into three portions. Dot one portion over the top two-thirds of the dough. Fold the bottom third up and the top third down over the butter. Seal the edges and turn so that the folded edges are at the sides. Roll into a rectangle again and repeat the process twice more. Cover the dough and leave in a cool place for 15 minutes. Roll out thinly and cut into triangles with 9in (22.5cm) long sides and 6in (15cm) base. Cut the chocolate into as many short thick bars as there are triangles.

Place a piece of chocolate at the base of each triangle and roll up loosely from the base. Curl the ends round to form a crescent. Place on baking trays and leave in a warm place for 20 minutes until well risen. Brush with beaten egg and bake at 450°F/230°C/Gas 8 for 10–15 minutes until golden brown. Eat freshly made.

9

SWEETMEATS AND PETITS FOURS

CHOCOLATE IS BOOMING. Everywhere there are chocolate shops together with grocers and gift shops with speciality chocolate departments. It is easy to buy luxury chocolates as presents or as self-indulgence, and after-dinner coffee is rarely served without some delectable sweetmeat. The traditional chocolate square allowed to children after a meal has been transformed into the adult truffle, liqueur cream or smooth fudge.

Sweet-making is a delicate art, but it is not difficult to acquire. For a few confections such as fudge, a sugar thermometer is useful, though not essential. Most sweetmeats rely on careful melting of the chocolate, a combination of the most delicious complementary flavours and long setting in a cool place. It is important not to over-handle chocolate sweetmeats as they quickly lose their shine and their charm, and they are best placed in paper or foil sweet cases as soon as they are prepared. Those who want to make very professional-looking sweets can now buy moulds and dipping tools in kitchen shops, so that little handling is required.

These sweetmeats are not designed to last a long time, and they are so good that they will get little chance to do so. Use the best possible chocolate, fresh cream, unsalted butter and good flavourings, and make only a small batch which will be eaten quickly.

Fresh Cream Truffles
★★

A light hand and scrupulous attention to detail will produce delectable truffles which must be eaten quickly.

Ingredients
FOR 1¼LB (550G) TRUFFLES (ABOUT 24)

¼pt (150ml) double cream
1 vanilla pod
1 egg yolk
1oz (25g) caster sugar
1lb (450g) plain chocolate
1oz (25g) unsalted butter
1 teasp oil

Put the cream and vanilla pod into a small, heavy-based pan and bring to the boil. Remove from the heat, cover and leave to stand for 20 minutes. Take out the vanilla pod (which may be washed, dried and used again). Put the egg yolk and caster sugar into a bowl and whisk until pale and thick. Whisk in the cream and return to the pan. Heat very gently for 3 minutes until the mixture begins to thicken, but do not boil. Break 5oz (125g) plain chocolate into small pieces. Take the cream off the heat and stir in the chocolate until melted. Chill in the refrigerator for 1 hour. Soften the butter and whisk into the mixture. Scoop out small spoonfuls of the mixture in rough truffle shapes and place on a piece of baking parchment. Freeze for 1 hour until very firm.

Break the remaining chocolate into a bowl over a pan of hot water and heat gently until melted. Stir in the oil. Remove from the heat and cool to lukewarm. Spoon a thin layer of chocolate over each truffle. When the chocolate has set firmly, turn the truffles over. Melt and cool any remaining chocolate and spoon over the base of each truffle to coat completely. Chill in the refrigerator and eat freshly made.

COOK'S TIP

For speed, or if a lighter Fresh Cream Truffle is preferred, only use 5oz (125g) chocolate from the ingredients. When the prepared mixture has been shaped and frozen, simply toss lightly in cocoa powder just before serving.

Liqueur Truffles
★★

Rich cream truffles flavoured with any favourite liqueur should be served freshly made.

Ingredients
FOR 24 TRUFFLES

8 tbs whipping cream
12oz (350g) plain chocolate
1oz (25g) unsalted butter
2 tbs liqueur

Put the cream into a heavy-based pan and heat gently to just below boiling point. Remove from the heat. Break half the chocolate into small pieces and stir into the cream with the butter. Beat well until smooth and thick. Cool to lukewarm and stir in the liqueur. Beat thoroughly and chill until firm. Shape the mixture into balls and chill again.

Break the remaining chocolate into small pieces and put into a bowl over hot water. Put a cocktail stick into each truffle. Remove the chocolate from heat and dip in each truffle. Drain well and fit sticks into a large potato or grapefruit. Leave until set and remove the cocktail sticks.

Double Truffles

❋❋

These truffles are a little fiddly to make but the contrast between the dark coating and creamy white interior is worth the trouble taken.

Ingredients
FOR 18 TRUFFLES

2 teasp liquid glucose
4 tbs double cream
5oz (125g) white chocolate

COATING

7oz (200g) plain chocolate
2oz (50g) unsalted butter
3 tbs double cream
2 tbs rum or Grand Marnier
cocoa powder

Put the glucose and cream into a small pan and bring to the boil. Take off the heat and stir in the white chocolate broken into small pieces. Stir until the chocolate has melted and then chill in the refrigerator until firm. Form into 18 small balls and chill until very firm.

To make the coating, put the chocolate and butter into a bowl over a pan of hot water and heat gently until the chocolate has melted. Take off the heat and stir well. Add the cream and rum or Grand Marnier. Chill until just firm. Form the mixture into 18 balls and flatten each ball into a round disc. Place a white chocolate ball in the centre of each one and wrap the dark coating round it. Roll lightly in cocoa powder, and chill for 3 hours until firm. Store in the refrigerator.

White Chocolate Truffles

❋❋

The sweet blandness of white chocolate is contrasted with kirsch and a mixture of fruit and nuts.

Ingredients
FOR 6OZ (175G) TRUFFLES (ABOUT 15)

4oz (100g) white chocolate
3 tbs double cream
2 tbs chopped mixed glacé fruit
1oz (25g) blanched split almonds
1 tbs kirsch
icing sugar

Chop the chocolate into small pieces. Put the cream and chocolate into a bowl over hot water and heat gently until the chocolate has melted. Meanwhile, chop the glacé fruit very finely. Spread the almonds on a baking sheet and toast under a medium grill until just golden. Chop the almonds finely and mix with the fruit. Stir into the chocolate and add the kirsch. Chill in the refrigerator for about 3 hours until firm. Roll into small balls with the hands, and roll lightly in icing sugar. Store in the refrigerator.

Parisian Truffles

Rich little truffles which are easily made for a dinner party.

Ingredients
For 8oz (225g) truffles (about 20)

4oz (100g) plain chocolate
4oz (100g) unsalted butter
2oz (50g) icing sugar
2 egg yolks
cocoa powder

Break the chocolate into small pieces and put into a bowl over a pan of hot water. Add the butter and heat gently until melted. Beat in the sugar and egg yolks, and continue cooking until thick. Cool and leave in a cold place overnight. Roll into small balls with the hands and roll lightly in cocoa powder. Store in the refrigerator.

Walnut Truffles

Slightly crunchy truffles which seem to melt in the mouth. Follow the method carefully or the sweets will be too sticky to roll successfully.

Ingredients
For 12oz (350g) truffles (about 30)

8oz (225g) plain chocolate
2oz (50g) unsalted butter
4 tbs double cream
2oz (50g) walnuts
2–3 tbs drinking chocolate powder

Break the chocolate into small pieces and put into a bowl over a pan of hot water.

Heat gently until just melted. Remove from the heat and stir in the butter and cream. Grind the walnuts in a blender and stir into the mixture. Leave until completely cold.

Scoop out teaspoonfuls of the mixture and form into balls with the hands. Place in a single layer on a sheet of baking parchment. Chill in the refrigerator and then roll the truffles lightly in drinking chocolate powder. Store in the refrigerator.

Chocolate Orange Truffles

Rich but delicate creamy truffles wrapped in dark chocolate.

Ingredients
For 12oz (350g) truffles (about 24)

4oz (100g) ground almonds
4oz (100g) icing sugar
1 tbs Cointreau or Grand Marnier
2 tbs double cream
6oz (150g) plain chocolate

Put the almonds into a bowl. Sieve in the icing sugar, and stir well until evenly coloured. Add the liqueur and cream and mix to a firm paste. Chill in the refrigerator for 20 minutes. Form into small balls. Break the chocolate into small pieces and put into a bowl over a pan of hot water. Heat gently until just melted. Use a teaspoon to dip the little balls until they are coated. Drain well and place on a sheet of baking parchment until cold and set. Place in paper sweet cases.

Rum and Almond Truffles

Quickly made truffles which are perfect with coffee after dinner.

Ingredients
FOR 18 TRUFFLES

4oz (100g) plain chocolate
4oz (100g) ground almonds
1oz (25g) caster sugar
2 tbs rum
2oz (50g) blanched almonds

Break the chocolate into small pieces and put into a bowl over a pan of hot water. Heat gently until the chocolate has melted. Stir in the almonds, sugar and rum. Remove from the heat and cool for 10 minutes. Roll into small balls. Chop the blanched almonds finely, and roll each truffle in the nuts. Chill for 30 minutes and put into sweet cases.

Rum Truffles

The flavouring may be varied by using brandy or an orange- or cherry-flavoured liqueur instead of rum.

Ingredients
FOR 12oz (350G) TRUFFLES (ABOUT 24)

8oz (225g) plain chocolate
2oz (50g) unsalted butter
1 tbs caster sugar
1 tbs rum
1 tbs double cream
1 egg yolk
cocoa or chocolate vermicelli

Break the chocolate into small pieces and put into a bowl over a pan of hot water. Heat gently until just melted. Take off the heat and stir in the butter, sugar, rum, cream and egg yolk. Beat until thick and cool. Put into the refrigerator for 20–30 minutes until firm but not hard. Shape into small balls and roll in cocoa or chocolate vermicelli. Place in paper sweet cases.

Rich Orange Truffles

Oranges and dark chocolate are natural companions, and in this recipe the truffles are richly flavoured with an orange liqueur, fresh orange rind and candied peel.

Ingredients
FOR 12oz (350G) TRUFFLES (ABOUT 30)

2oz (50g) unsalted butter
5 tbs double cream
7oz (200g) plain chocolate
1 egg yolk
2 tbs chopped mixed candied peel
2 tbs Grand Marnier or Cointreau
1 teasp grated orange rind
cocoa powder

Cut the butter into small pieces and put into a small, heavy-based pan with the cream. Heat gently until the butter has melted and the cream is bubbling. Take off heat and add the chocolate broken into small pieces. Leave until the chocolate has melted and stir well. Mix in the egg yolk. Chop the peel very finely and stir into the mixture with the liqueur and orange rind. Chill in the refrigerator for about 3 hours until firm. Roll into small balls with the hands. Roll lightly in cocoa powder and chill before serving. Store in the refrigerator.

Chocolate Fudge

Chocolate fudge is always delicious, but extra flavour may be added with nuts, dried fruit or a little rum.

Ingredients

FOR 1½LB (675G) FUDGE

1lb (450g) sugar
6fl oz (175ml) milk
2oz (50g) plain chocolate
2oz (50g) unsalted butter
few drops of vanilla essence

Put the sugar and milk into a thick-based pan. Chop the chocolate finely and add to the milk. Stir over a low heat until the chocolate and sugar have melted. Boil gently to 237°F/114°C (or until a little of the mixture dropped into a cup of cold water forms a soft ball), stirring occasionally to prevent burning.

Take off the heat and add the butter. Cool for 5 minutes and beat hard with a wooden spoon until the mixture loses its gloss. Pour quickly into an oiled 11x7in (27.5x17.5cm) tin. Mark into squares while still slightly soft. Leave until cold before cutting and removing from the tin.

Chocolate Cinnamon Fudge

A rich fudge in which the chocolate is spiked with cinnamon to make a very sophisticated sweetmeat.

Ingredients

FOR 2LB (900G) FUDGE

1½lb (675g) sugar
½pt (300ml) milk
6oz (175g) plain chocolate
4½oz (115g) unsalted butter
1½ teasp ground cinnamon

Put the sugar and milk into a heavy-based pan. Break the chocolate into small pieces and add to the pan with the butter. Heat gently until the sugar has dissolved, stirring well. Boil gently to 237°F/114°C (or until a little of the mixture dropped into a cup of cold water forms a soft ball), stirring occasionally to prevent burning.

Take off the heat and cool for 5 minutes. Add the cinnamon and beat hard with a wooden spoon until the mixture loses its gloss. Pour quickly into an oiled 11x7in (27.5x17.5cm) tin. Mark into squares while still slightly soft. Leave until set before cutting and removing from the tin.

Uncooked Chocolate Fudge

★

A fudge for fainthearts who are worried about boiling sugar. This fudge stores well in a freezer and is useful for holiday periods.

Ingredients
For 2lb (900g) fudge

8oz (225g) plain chocolate
4oz (100g) unsalted butter
1 egg
1lb (450g) icing sugar
4 tbs sweetened condensed milk or double cream

Break the chocolate into small pieces and put into a bowl with the butter over a pan of hot water. Heat gently until melted. Beat the egg lightly in a bowl. Sieve the icing sugar and add gradually to the egg with the milk or cream and the chocolate mixture. Beat well and put into a lightly buttered 11x7in (27.5x17.5cm) tin. Chill in the refrigerator for 3 hours until firm and cut into squares. Store in the refrigerator or freezer.

For ease of freezer storage, pour the mixture into rigid non-metal containers and do not mark into squares. Cover with foil or a freezer bag for storage up to 3 months.

If liked, chopped nuts, dried fruit or grated orange rind may be added to the fudge.

Chocolate Orange Creams

★★

Squares of creamy orange chocolate are easily made and are very good with coffee after dinner.

Ingredients
For 1¼lb (550g) squares (about 40)

3oz (75g) caster sugar
2 egg yolks
2oz (50g) unsalted butter
4 tbs double cream
juice of ½ orange
1 teasp grated orange rind
1lb (450g) plain chocolate
2oz (50g) candied orange peel

Put the sugar and egg yolks into a bowl and whisk together until light and creamy. Put over a pan of hot water and stir in the butter, cream, orange juice and rind. Stir over heat until thick, but do not let the mixture boil. Break 8oz (225g) chocolate into small pieces and stir into the mixture. When the chocolate has melted, stir in the finely chopped candied peel. Line an 8x10in (20x25cm) tin with baking parchment. Pour the mixture into the tin and leave until cold and set. Turn out on to a clean sheet of baking parchment and peel off the lining paper.

Break the remaining chocolate into small pieces and put into a bowl over hot water. Heat until just melted. Leave to cool for 5 minutes and then spread over the chocolate cream. Leave until set and mark into small squares. When completely cold and firm, cut into squares and place in paper sweet cases.

Praline Log
★★

A mocha truffle mixture is formed into a log and then rolled in crushed almond praline before being cut into tempting slices.

Ingredients
FOR 1LB (450G) SWEETS

6oz (175g) plain chocolate
3oz (75g) unsalted butter
1oz (25g) caster sugar
1 tbs strong black coffee
1 tbs brandy
1 egg and 1 egg yolk

PRALINE

3oz (75g) blanched almonds
4oz (100g) sugar
4 tbs water

Break the chocolate into small pieces and put into a bowl with the butter, sugar, coffee and brandy. Put the bowl over a pan of hot water and heat gently until the chocolate has melted. Take off the heat and cool for 5 minutes. Separate the egg and beat the two yolks into the chocolate mixture. Beat the egg white to stiff peaks and fold in. Cool and then chill for 3 hours. Shape into a log 2in (5cm) in diameter and chill again.

While the mixture is chilling, prepare the praline. Put the nuts on to a baking sheet and bake at 350°F/180°C/Gas 4 for 5 minutes. Put the sugar and water into a heavy-based pan and heat gently until the sugar has dissolved. Bring to the boil and cool to a light caramel colour. Stir in the nuts. Butter a 10in (25cm) tin or a marble slab. Pour the mixture into the tin or on to the slab. Leave until cold and break into pieces. Crush in a food processor or with a rolling pin, but do not reduce to powder.

Roll the chilled log in the praline to make a thick coating, and chill again until needed. Slice into about 30 pieces.

Chocolate Torrone
★★

A fudge-like sweetmeat containing crisp little nuggets of biscuit.

Ingredients
FOR 12OZ (350G) TORRONE

4oz (100g) plain chocolate
4oz (100g) unsalted butter
2 tbs icing sugar
2 tbs rum
2 eggs
2oz (50g) ground almonds
4 tbs broken Petit Beurre biscuits

Line a 1lb (450g) loaf tin with foil, and brush lightly with oil.

Break the chocolate into a bowl over a pan of hot water and heat gently until melted. Remove from the heat and leave to cool to lukewarm. Cream the butter and sugar until light and fluffy and work in the rum. Separate the eggs and beat the yolks into the mixture. Stir in the ground almonds, and gradually beat in the chocolate.

Whisk the egg whites to stiff peaks and fold into the mixture. Break the biscuits into pieces about the size of a pea and stir into the mixture. Put into the prepared tin and smooth the surface. Cover and chill in the refrigerator for 6 hours. Turn out on to a flat surface and cut into slices, then cut each slice in half. Store in the refrigerator.

Colettes

★★

Classic chocolate creams to serve with coffee. They will store in the refrigerator for up to 7 days.

Ingredients
FOR 24 COLETTES

1lb (450g) plain chocolate
¼pt (150ml) double cream
2 tbs rum or brandy
2oz (50g) unsalted butter
24 hazelnuts

Take 48 paper sweet cases and put them together in pairs to make 24 thicker containers. Take 6oz (175g) chocolate and put into a bowl over a pan of hot water. When the chocolate has melted, stir well and remove from the heat. Spread chocolate on the base and sides of the paper cases to form an interior chocolate case. Place on a tray and chill in the refrigerator until set. Put the cream into a bowl over a pan of hot water. When the cream is almost boiling, add the remaining chocolate broken into small pieces. Stir until the chocolate has melted. Add the rum or brandy and butter, and continue stirring over hot water until the mixture is thick and smooth. Take off heat and leave until cool. Put into a piping bag fitted with a large star nozzle and pipe a whorl of chocolate cream into each case. Place a hazelnut on each one. Store in the refrigerator.

Chocolate Snaps

★★

Tiny chocolate biscuit cones filled with chocolate liqueur cream are an exciting addition to the *petits fours* selection. If cream horn moulds are not available, roll the mixture round oiled wooden spoon handles like brandy snaps.

Ingredients
FOR 15 SNAPS

1oz (25g) plain chocolate
1oz (25g) unsalted butter
2 tbs light soft brown sugar
1½ tbs clear honey
1oz (25g) plain flour

FILLING

¼pt (150ml) double cream
1 tbs orange liqueur
1 tbs icing sugar
2oz (50g) plain chocolate

Preheat the oven to 350°F/180°C/Gas 4. Cover two baking sheets with baking-parchment. Put the chocolate, butter, sugar and honey into a small, heavy-based pan and heat gently until melted. Take off the heat and work in the flour. Drop teaspoonfuls of mixture on to the baking parchment, leaving room for spreading (for ease of working, bake only 2–3 snaps on each sheet at a time). Bake for 5 minutes until just setting round edges. Leave on the tray for 30 seconds, lift off with a palette knife and wrap at once around the base of cream horn tins. When cold and crisp, slip off the moulds. If liked, the snaps may be stored in an airtight tin for 24 hours before filling.

To make the filling, whip the cream, liqueur and icing sugar to soft peaks. Melt the chocolate in a bowl over hot water, cool and stir into the cream. Just before serving, pipe the chocolate cream into the biscuit cases.

Chocolate Almond Crunch

**

Rich coffee-flavoured toffee packed with toasted almonds is covered with chocolate and more nuts.

Ingredients

FOR 1½LB (675G) TOFFEE

6oz (175g) blanched split almonds
8oz (225g) caster sugar
6oz (175g) unsalted butter
1 tbs coffee powder
1 tbs boiling water
4oz (100g) plain chocolate

Place the almonds in a thin layer on a baking sheet and toast under a medium grill until just tinged with gold. Chop 2oz (50g) almonds and keep on one side. Put the sugar and butter into a thick-based pan. Dissolve the coffee in the water and add to the pan. Heat gently, stirring all the time until the sugar has dissolved. Boil gently to 280°F/138°C (or until a little of the mixture dropped into a cup of cold water separates into threads which are hard but not brittle).

Take off the heat and stir in the split almonds. Pour into an oiled baking tin and leave until cold. Put the chocolate into a bowl over a pan of hot water and heat until melted. Spread the chocolate over the toffee and sprinkle with chopped almonds. Leave until set and break the toffee into pieces.

Chocolate Cherry Creams

**

These *petits fours* take a little care and time to make, but the results are delicious.

Ingredients

FOR 24 CHOCOLATES

24 maraschino cherries
4 tbs brandy
8oz (225g) plain chocolate
2oz (50g) sugar
2 tbs water
2oz (50g) unsalted butter
2oz (50g) icing sugar

Put the cherries into a bowl and cover with the brandy. Leave to stand for 8 hours. Take 48 paper sweet cases and put them together in pairs to make 24 firmer cases. Break the chocolate into small pieces and put half of it into a bowl over a pan of hot water. Heat gently until just melted. Brush the chocolate fairly thickly inside the sweet cases to cover the sides and bases completely. Leave until cold and set.

Drain the cherries and place one in each chocolate case. Put the sugar and water into a thick-based pan and boil to a thick syrup. Add half the drained brandy, stir well and cool. Cover the cherries with this syrup. Cream the butter and icing sugar and remaining brandy, and pipe this mixture over the cherries. Chill in the refrigerator until cold and firm.

Grate 1oz (25g) chocolate and keep on one side. Melt the remaining chocolate over hot water, leave until almost cold, and pour over the sweets. Sprinkle with grated chocolate. Leave until cold and set before removing from the paper cases.

Crazy Pavement

Quickly made and delicious, this sweet-meat provides a contrast of flavours and textures as well as colours.

Ingredients

FOR 1¼LB (550G) SWEETS

1lb (450g) plain chocolate
12 pink and white marshmallows
3oz (75g) walnuts
3oz (75g) seedless raisins

Break the chocolate into small pieces and put into a bowl over a pan of hot water. Heat gently until just melted. Chop the marshmallows with kitchen scissors. Chop the walnuts roughly.

Line a baking tray with baking parchment. Remove the chocolate from the heat and stir in the marshmallows, raisins and walnuts until well coated. Pour into the tin and smooth evenly. Leave until cold and hard, and break into pieces.

Chocolate Pralines

Creamy nutty little chocolates which are an attractive addition to a dish of *petits fours*.

Ingredients

FOR 18 PRALINES

4oz (100g) plain chocolate
2oz (50g) unsalted butter
3oz (75g) icing sugar
1oz (25g) ground hazelnuts
1 teasp rum or coffee liqueur
18 crystallised violets

Break the chocolate into small pieces and put into a bowl with the butter. Place over a pan of hot water and heat gently until just melted. Remove from the heat and stir in the sugar, nuts and liqueur. Beat well and then put the mixture into a piping bag fitted with a star nozzle. Place 18 paper sweet cases on a plate and pipe the mixture in a whorl into each case. Top with a crystallised violet. Chill in the refrigerator for 30 minutes and serve freshly made.

Chocolate Strawberries

A colourful way of combining the sharpness of fruit with the smooth richness of chocolate makes *petits fours* for the end of a summer meal or a wedding reception.

Ingredients

FOR 1LB (450G) *petits fours*

6oz (175g) plain chocolate
1½oz (40g) unsalted butter
6 tbs double cream
1lb (450g) strawberries

Use fresh, ripe, firm strawberries and make sure that they are very clean and dry; leave the green tops in place. Put the chocolate into a bowl with the butter over a pan of hot water. Heat gently until the chocolate has melted. Take off the heat and stir in the cream. Leave until cool and just beginning to thicken.

Place a piece of baking parchment on a flat surface. Hold each strawberry by its stalk and dip into the chocolate until two-thirds covered. Place on the baking parchment. Leave until completely cold and firm. Lift off the paper and arrange on a serving dish.

Orange Thins

Flavoured chocolate morsels to serve with after-dinner coffee.

Ingredients
For 10oz (300g) sweets

8oz (225g) plain chocolate
2oz (50g) unsalted butter
1 teasp grated orange rind
2 tbs orange liqueur

Line an 8in (20cm) square cake tin with foil and brush the foil lightly with flavourless oil. Put the chocolate and butter into a bowl over a pan of hot water and heat gently until just melted. Remove from the heat and stir in the orange rind and liqueur. Pour into the lined tin. Cover and chill until set. Turn out of the pan and cut into squares or triangles. Keep in the refrigerator before serving.

Coffee Thins Substitute 1 teasp instant coffee powder and 2 tbs coffee liqueur for the orange rind and liqueur.

Chocolate Coconut Ice

Coconut ice is a very old-fashioned sweetmeat but is rather unusual when flavoured with chocolate.

Ingredients
Makes 1¼lb (550g) coconut ice

1lb (450g) granulated sugar
¼pt (150ml) milk
2 tbs cocoa powder
4oz (100g) desiccated coconut

Put the sugar, milk and cocoa powder into a heavy saucepan. Stir well and boil for 5 minutes. Take off the heat and stir in the coconut. Beat hard for 1 minute and pour into a tin rinsed in cold water. Leave until cold before cutting into squares or bars.

Chocolate Crunchies

Quickly-made little sweets which store well in a tin.

Ingredients
For 1lb (450g) sweets (about 20)

8oz (225g) plain chocolate
2oz (50g) glacé cherries
2oz (50g) angelica
2oz (50g) sultanas
2oz (50g) seedless raisins
2oz (50g) walnuts

Break the chocolate into small pieces and put into a bowl over a pan of hot water. Heat gently until just melted. Chop all the other ingredients roughly. Remove the chocolate from the heat and stir in the fruit and nuts. Drop spoonfuls into paper sweet cases and leave until set.

10
SAUCES

A SMOOTH SAUCE provides a professional finish to a dish, producing a flavour which intensifies or enhances a pudding, a texture which adds richness and a colour which improves appearances. Even simple custard or flavoured cream can provide the perfect partner for a chocolate pudding. On the other hand a very dark and syrupy chocolate sauce, coffee sauce or a contrasting fruit sauce will provide a most sophisticated blending of flavours, colours and textures. Try a sauce with almost any hot or cold pudding or ice – even mousses and soufflés benefit from the contrast. Chocolate addicts may care to make up a large quantity of chocolate sauce and store it in the refrigerator or freezer to use with everything.

Chocolate Sauce
*

A quickly made sauce which is richly flavoured and glossy. It will thicken as it cools, and should be stirred occasionally. Serve it hot or cold, or store in the freezer for emergencies.

Ingredients
For 4–6

¼pt (150ml) water
4oz (100g) caster sugar
2oz (50g) cocoa powder

Put the water and sugar into a pan and heat gently until the sugar has dissolved. Bring to the boil and simmer for 1 minute. Whisk in the cocoa and bring back to the boil, whisking hard until the sauce is smooth.

Mocha Cream Sauce
*

This rich, creamy chocolate sauce spiked with coffee and brandy may be served hot or cold.

Ingredients
For ¾pt (450ml) sauce

½pt (300ml) double cream
1 tbs strong black coffee
8oz (225g) plain chocolate
1 tbs brandy

Put the cream and coffee into a heavy-based pan and bring just to the boil. Break the chocolate into small pieces and add to the pan. Heat gently until the chocolate has melted. Take off the heat and add the brandy, stirring until smooth.

Mocha Sauce

Coffee-spiked chocolate sauce which will pair with mocha puddings or with chocolate ones.

Ingredients
FOR 4

1oz (25g) butter
1oz (25g) plain flour
¾pt (450ml) milk
1 tbs coffee essence
2oz (50g) plain chocolate
1 tbs caster sugar

Put the butter into a pan and heat gently until melted. Stir in the flour and cook for 1 minute over low heat. Work in the milk and stir over low heat until smooth and creamy. Stir in the coffee essence and cook for 1 minute. Chop the chocolate finely and add to the sauce with the sugar. Stir until melted and serve at once. For added richness, stir 2–3 tbs cream into the sauce just before serving.

Chocolate Whipped Custard

A light chocolate custard, which is very good with steamed puddings.

Ingredients
FOR 4

½pt (300ml) milk
1 tbs caster sugar
1 egg
1oz (25g) plain chocolate

Put the milk and sugar into a small pan and bring to boiling point. Separate the egg and put the yolk into a bowl. Pour on a little of the hot milk and beat well. Strain back into the pan with the remaining milk and stir gently over low heat until thickened. Chop the chocolate finely and stir into the custard. Remove from the heat and cool slightly. Whisk the egg white to soft peaks and fold into the custard. Serve at once.

Chocolate Mousseline Sauce

*R*ich creamy sauce to serve with pancakes or light sponge puddings.

Ingredients
FOR 4

2 eggs and 1 egg yolk
2½fl oz (65ml) double cream
1½oz (40g) caster sugar
2 tbs sweet sherry
2oz (50g) grated plain chocolate

Put the eggs and egg yolk into a bowl with the cream, and place over a pan of hot water. Heat gently, beating until smooth and thick. Add the sugar and sherry and beat until the sugar has melted. Stir in the chocolate and remove from the heat.

Chocolate Mousse Sauce

---*---

A rich, foaming sauce for ices, mousses and puddings.

Ingredients
FOR 4

4oz (100g) plain chocolate
1oz (25g) butter
6 tbs water
2 eggs

Put the chocolate into a bowl with the butter and water and heat over a pan of hot water until just melted. Separate the eggs. Remove chocolate from heat and beat in the egg yolks. Whisk the egg whites to soft peaks and fold into the mixture. Serve at once.

Dark Chocolate Rum Sauce

---*---

Luscious chocolate sauce to serve with hot puddings or with ice cream. If preferred, strong coffee may be used instead of water and the rum omitted.

Ingredients
FOR 4–6

2oz (50g) caster sugar
4 tbs water
4oz (100g) plain chocolate
2 tbs rum
1/2oz (15g) unsalted butter

Put the sugar and water into a small, heavy-based pan over low heat and stir until the sugar has dissolved. Bring to the boil. Take off the heat and add small pieces of chocolate, stirring well. Stir in the rum and butter and serve at once.

Chocolate Butterscotch Sauce

---*---

A lightly flavoured chocolate sauce which is good with steamed or baked puddings or vanilla ice cream.

Ingredients
FOR 1/2PT (300ML) SAUCE

2oz (50g) unsalted butter
2oz (50g) demerara sugar
1oz (25g) drinking chocolate powder
6fl oz (175ml) creamy milk

Mix the butter, sugar and drinking chocolate powder in a heavy-based pan, and stir over low heat until the butter has melted and the sugar has dissolved. Raise the heat and cook for 2 minutes. Take off the heat and stir in the milk until evenly blended. Bring to the boil and cook for 2 minutes. Serve warm or cold.

Chocolate Fudge Sauce
*

A good sauce to serve hot or warm over puddings, mousses or ices.

Ingredients
½PT (300ML) SAUCE

6oz (175g) can evaporated milk
3oz (75g) plain chocolate
2oz (50g) light soft brown sugar
1oz (25g) butter
¼ teasp vanilla essence

Put the evaporated milk into a heavy-based pan. Break the chocolate into small pieces and add to the pan with the sugar and butter. Heat gently and stir continuously over low heat until the chocolate has melted and the sugar has dissolved, but do not boil. Remove from the heat and stir in the vanilla essence.

Mint Cream
*

A perfect filling for chocolate pancakes or topping for a rich chocolate mousse or gâteau.

Ingredients
FOR ½PT (300ML) CREAM

½pt (300ml) double cream
1 tbs caster sugar
3 tbs crème de menthe

Whip the cream to soft peaks. Add the sugar and continue whipping until the cream stands in stiff peaks. Stir in the crème de menthe until evenly coloured.

Coffee Custard Sauce
**

Coffee is the perfect complement to chocolate, and this rich custard is good with any dark chocolate pudding, whether hot or cold.

Ingredients
FOR 1PT (600ML) SAUCE

½pt (300ml) milk
½pt (300ml) single cream
1oz (25g) coffee powder
4 egg yolks
3oz (75g) caster sugar

Put the milk, cream and coffee powder into a heavy-based pan and bring to the boil. Whisk the egg yolks and sugar in a bowl until thick and creamy. Slowly pour the milk on to the eggs, whisking all the time. Return to the pan and stir gently over low heat until the mixture thickens and coats the back of a spoon. Strain and serve hot or cold.

Mars Bar Sauce
*

The secret treat of generations of bed-sitter dwellers, this instant chocolate sauce tastes wonderful over ice creams and puddings. Simply chop two large Mars Bars and heat very gently in a small, heavy-based saucepan. When melted, stir well and use at once. For incredible richness, stir in a spoonful or two of thick cream just before serving.

Raspberry Liqueur Sauce

Clear red fruit sauce is quickly made and provides a wonderful foil to chocolate dishes. Framboise, kirsch, cassis, rum or brandy may be used for the alcoholic content.

Ingredients

For ½pt (300ml) sauce

1lb (450g) fresh or frozen raspberries
8oz (225g) icing sugar
juice of ½ lemon
2 tbs liqueur

Sieve the fruit to make a purée. Stir in the sugar and lemon juice until the sugar has dissolved. Chill and stir in the liqueur just before serving.

Orange Sauce

Oranges go beautifully with chocolate, and this sauce helps to offset the richness of hot chocolate puddings.

Ingredients

For ½pt (300ml) sauce

2 oranges
½pt (300ml) water
1 tbs unsalted butter
1 tbs plain flour
½oz (15g) caster sugar
2 tbs orange liqueur

Grate the rind of the oranges and put into a heavy-based pan with the water. Bring to the boil and simmer for 10 minutes. In another pan, melt the butter and work in the flour. Add the orange liqueur and simmer for 5 minutes, stirring well. Squeeze the juice from the oranges and strain into the pan. Add the sugar, stir well and simmer over low heat for 5 minutes. Remove from the heat and stir in the liqueur. Serve at once.

Crème Anglaise

The French version of custard is thin, sweet and creamy, and is delicious cold with chocolate dishes.

Ingredients

For 1pt (600ml) sauce

½pt (300ml) milk
vanilla pod
6 egg yolks
4oz (100g) caster sugar
½pt (300ml) single cream
2 teasp orange flower water

Put the milk into a heavy-based pan with the split vanilla pod. Bring to the boil. Take off the heat, cover and leave to stand for 10 minutes. Whisk the yolks and sugar together in a bowl until pale and creamy. Strain in the milk, whisking well. Put into a heavy-based pan and stir over low heat until the sauce coats the spoon. Remove from the heat and leave to cool, stirring frequently. When nearly cold, stir in the cream and orange flower water.

11

DRINKS

CHOCOLATE IS AN ALMOST universal comforter. There is nothing quite like a hot or cold chocolate drink to comfort, feed and yet stimulate. In warmer countries such as Mexico, they like their chocolate spiked with spices or contrasting coffee; in colder climates, the chocolate has to be lighter, sweeter and frothier, often served with cream or laced with spirits.

A smooth chocolate syrup is a good basis for cold chocolate drinks, quickly prepared with chilled milk or ice cream. For hot drinks, cocoa powder or drinking chocolate powder is now most easily used, although they were once prepared with melted, unsweetened chocolate in a long and laborious business.

Chocolate Nog
★

An old-fashioned way of making a nourishing milk drink for a cold morning.

Ingredients
FOR 2

¾pt (450ml) milk
1 tbs caster sugar
1 vanilla pod
1 egg
3oz (75g) plain chocolate

Put the milk, caster sugar and vanilla pod into a heavy-based pan and heat gently. When the milk is just at boiling point, remove from heat and take out the vanilla pod (this can be washed, dried and used again). Separate the egg, and whisk the egg yolk and milk together. Break the chocolate into small pieces and add to the mixture, stirring until creamy. Whisk the egg white to stiff peaks. Pour in the hot milk, whisking all the time. Pour into 2 warm mugs and serve at once. If liked, a blob of whipped cream may be placed on top of each serving.

Real Cocoa

* * *

Real men like real cocoa, made in the traditional way, preferably with Dutch cocoa powder, which has the finest flavour.

Ingredients

FOR 4

4 tbs cocoa powder
3 tbs sugar
pinch of salt
¼pt (150ml) boiling water
1½pt (900ml) milk

Mix the cocoa powder, sugar and salt in a heavy-based pan. Add the water and mix to a paste. Simmer for 3 minutes. Add the milk and heat slowly to just below boiling point. Whisk well and pour into hot mugs. If you are a sailor or wildfowler, add some rum.

Basic Chocolate Syrup

* * *

This syrup may be used as a sauce for puddings and ice creams, but it is useful to store in the refrigerator as the base for chocolate drinks.

Ingredients

FOR ½PT (300ML) SYRUP

½pt (300ml) water
10oz (300g) light soft brown sugar
4oz (100g) cocoa powder
pinch of salt
2 teasp vanilla essence

Put the water into a heavy-based pan and stir in the sugar, cocoa powder and salt.

Bring to the boil and then simmer for 5 minutes, stirring often. Remove from the heat and leave to cool, stirring occasionally. Stir in the vanilla essence. When cold, cover and store in the refrigerator.

Chocolate Toddy

* * *

A soothing bedtime drink with a very special flavour.

Ingredients

FOR 2

1pt (600ml) milk
2oz (50g) plain chocolate
2–3 tbs rum
1 tbs double cream
pinch of ground nutmeg

Put the milk into a heavy-based pan. Break the chocolate into small pieces and add to the pan. Bring to the boil, stirring occasionally. Take off the heat and stir in the rum. Divide between two warm mugs. Pour the cream over the back of a teaspoon on to the hot chocolate, so that the cream floats on the surface. Sprinkle lightly with nutmeg and serve at once.

Swiss Chocolate

Richly warming and comforting, this is the drink for a cold winter's night, or even for mid-morning after a brisk walk.

Ingredients

FOR 4

2pt (1.2l) milk
4 heaped tbs drinking chocolate powder
¼pt (150ml) double cream
pinch of ground cinnamon or cocoa powder

Heat the milk to boiling point. Take off heat and whisk in the drinking chocolate powder. Whip the cream to soft peaks. Pour the hot chocolate into mugs. Spoon cream on top of each mug and sprinkle lightly with cinnamon or cocoa powder.

Breakfast Chocolate

Thick hot chocolate makes a marvellous drink for a winter breakfast, to accompany croissants, brioches or a lightly fruited bun.

Ingredients

FOR 2

3oz (75g) plain chocolate
5 tbs boiling water
½pt (300ml) creamy milk

Break the chocolate into small pieces and put into a heavy-based pan with the water. Heat gently, stirring well, until the chocolate has melted and the mixture is thick. Heat the milk in another saucepan. Divide the hot chocolate between two mugs and pour in the hot milk. Serve at once.

Mexican Chocolate

Almost a complete meal, this spiced chocolate drink is very reviving in cold weather.

Ingredients

FOR 4

1pt (600ml) milk
½pt (300ml) double cream
½ teasp ground cinnamon
½ teasp ground nutmeg
pinch of ground allspice
pinch of salt
2oz (50g) plain chocolate
5 tbs water
2 egg yolks

Put the milk and cream into a bowl over a pan of hot water and bring just to the boil. Add the spices and salt, and simmer for 1 hour.

Just before serving, heat the chocolate and water in a small pan over low heat until the chocolate has melted. Take off the heat and beat in the egg yolks. Whisk in the spiced milk until the mixture thickens. Serve at once.

Chocolate Ice Cream Soda

⋆

A quickly assembled summer drink, which is easily made if all the ingredients have been well chilled in the refrigerator. The ice cream may be chocolate, vanilla or mint-flavoured.

Ingredients
FOR 1

3 tbs Chocolate Syrup (p116)
1 tbs double cream
1 scoop ice cream
soda water

Put the Chocolate Syrup and cream into a tall glass and stir until well mixed. Add the ice cream and top up with soda water. Stir thoroughly and serve at once with a straw and long spoon.

Mocha Cooler

⋆

A treat for a hot day which is filling enough to serve instead of a meal.

Ingredients
FOR 4

1pt (600ml) strong black coffee
2oz (50g) plain chocolate
8 scoops coffee ice cream

Make the coffee freshly and leave it to cool. Break the chocolate into small pieces and put into a basin over hot water. Heat until melted and then leave to cool.

Just before serving, put the coffee and chocolate into a blender and mix well. Add the ice cream and blend until thick and creamy. Pour into tall glasses and serve with straws.

Chocolate Milk Shake

⋆

Refreshing milk shakes are best made with milk which has been chilled in the refrigerator and whirled up in a blender with flavouring.

Ingredients
FOR 1

½pt (300ml) milk
3 tbs Chocolate Syrup (p116)
2 tbs finely crushed ice
pinch of ground cinnamon or nutmeg

Put the milk, Chocolate Syrup and ice into a blender and whirl until well mixed. Pour into a chilled glass and sprinkle with cinnamon or nutmeg.

Iced Chocolate

A refreshing but nourishing drink for a hot day. The syrup may be prepared in advance and stored in the refrigerator for a day or two.

Ingredients
For 4–6

8oz (225g) caster sugar
½pt (300ml) water
2oz (50g) cocoa powder
1 teasp coffee powder
2pt (1.2l) chilled milk

Put the sugar and water into a heavy-based pan and heat gently until the sugar has dissolved. Bring to the boil, but do not stir, and boil for about 5 minutes to make a thin syrup. Remove from the heat and whisk in the cocoa powder and coffee powder until there are no lumps. Refurn to low heat and simmer for 3 minutes. Pour into a jug and chill in the refrigerator. Whisk in the chilled milk just before serving.

Chocolate Liègeois

The richest chocolate drink, which may be served at the end of a meal instead of a pudding and coffee.

Ingredients
For 4

¼pt (150ml) Chocolate Syrup (p116)
1pt (600ml) creamy milk
4 scoops chocolate or vanilla ice cream
¼pt (150ml) double cream
2 teasp caster sugar
cocoa powder

Mix the Chocolate Syrup and milk until evenly coloured and pour into four tall chilled glasses. Add a scoop of ice cream to each glass. Whip the cream and sugar to stiff peaks and divide among the glasses. Sprinkle lightly with cocoa powder and serve at once with straws and long spoons.

12

FANCY BITS

SINCE MOST CHOCOLATE DISHES are very dark in colour, they can also appear flat and dull. Their appearance is greatly enhanced by the addition of smooth, shiny chocolate decorations which are easily prepared.

Squares, Triangles and Other Shapes

Melt plain chocolate and spread thinly with a palette knife on a completely flat sheet of baking parchment. Leave to set at room temperature until firm but not brittle. Use a sharp knife to cut squares or triangles, or use cake or cocktail cutters for circles and other shapes. Lift carefully from the baking parchment. Any offcuts may be melted and used again.

Leaves

Choose fresh leaves which are not poisonous and which have an attractive shape and prominent veining (rose leaves are ideal). Wash and dry the leaves thoroughly. Brush one surface of each leaf thickly and evenly with melted chocolate, preferably using the heavily veined side. Arrange on a sheet of baking parchment and leave until the chocolate is hard. Peel off the leaves carefully.

Lace

Draw triangles or circles on baking parchment. Put melted chocolate into a small piping bag with a small writing pipe and pipe round the outline of each shape. Fill in with lacy lines. Leave to set at room temperature. Lift very carefully from the paper.

Palm Trees

Use a small piping bag with a writing pipe, and fill with melted chocolate. Pipe a six-pointed starfish shape on to baking parchment. Pipe on a trunk from the centre, giving a ringed effect by using short horizontal lines. Leave to set at room temperature.

Caraque (Long Curls)

Melt plain chocolate and spread with a palette knife less than ¼in (5mm) thick on clean dry marble or a laminated surface. Leave to set at room temperature. Using a long knife, hold the blade at an angle of 45° to the surface and push away from the body, shaving off long curls. Lift off carefully with a skewer or pointed knife. Small flakes which break off may also be used as decoration or may be melted and used again.

Short Curls

Use a thick block of plain chocolate or cake covering, as French cooking chocolate is too hard and brittle for this technique. Use at room temperature, and scrape off curls of chocolate with a potato peeler (the type with a light, thin rotary blade is easiest to use). Do not handle the curls which melt easily, but lift them with the point of a knife directly on to the surface to be decorated.

Grated Chocolate

Use a thick block of plain chocolate or cake covering and chill for 30 minutes in the refrigerator. Use the coarse side of the grater for preparing the chocolate.

Chocolate Horns

Use cream-horn tins which have been washed and dried. Rub the insides with kitchen paper to make them shiny. Pour in melted chocolate and tilt the horn moulds so that the inside is evenly coated. Leave to set and then repeat the process to make a thicker casing which will be easier to unmould. Leave to set in a cool place and when the chocolate has set hard, ease out with the point of a knife. For small horns which are suitable for *petits fours*, paint the chocolate only a short way up the outside of the horn moulds. Leave to set and repeat the process. When the chocolate is hard, slip it out of the moulds.

Cake and Sweet Bases

Put together paper or foil cake or sweet cases in pairs to provide a firm base. Paint chocolate thinly inside the inner case to cover completely. Leave until hard and then repeat the process. When the chocolate has set, peel off the outer cases and use the chocolate shapes for filling with liqueurs, truffle mixture, soft fruit, fondant, etc.

LIST OF RECIPES

Sweetmeats and Petits Fours

Sauces

Drinks

INDEX